RELIC QUEST

RoBeRT CoRNuKe

TYNDALE HOUSE PUBLISHERS, INC., WHEATON, ILLINOIS

Visit Tyndale's exciting Web site at www.tyndale.com

TYNDALE is a registered trademark of Tyndale House Publishers, Inc.

Tyndale's quill logo is a trademark of Tyndale House Publishers, Inc.

Relic Quest

Designed by Luke Daab

Edited by Linda Schlafer

Library of Congress Cataloging-in-Publication Data

Cornuke, Robert, date.
  Relic quest / Robert Cornuke.
    p. cm.
  ISBN-13: 978-1-4143-0297-3 (pbk.)
  ISBN-10: 1-4143-0297-5 (pbk.)
    1. Bible. O.T. Exodus—Antiquities. 2. Cornuke, Robert, 1951—Travel. 3. Ark of the Covenant. I. Title.
  BS1245.55.C67 2005
  222'.12093—dc22

                            2005001425

Printed in the United States of America

11 10 09 08 07 06 05
7   6   5   4   3   2   1

To Terry and our wonderful children.
You are the unabated joy that carries me on.

"Man must explore."

Apollo 15 astronaut David R. Scott, from the surface of the moon, 1971

CONTENTS

ACKNOWLEDGMENTS

With a project of this magnitude, there are many people to thank. Although I am unable to list every name, I hope that everyone knows how deeply I appreciate their contributions to this book.

A few are deserving of special mention. David Halbrook, your words have their fingerprints all over this manuscript. Dr. Roy Knuteson, your research pointed the way. Ken Durham and Graham Hancock, your theories opened darkened vaults in time. Jim Irwin, you inspired me beyond the limits of my self-imposed borders. Larry Williams, your courage dwarfs mine. Mary Irwin, your words have renewed my soul. Doug Sherling and Steve Crampton, your friendship goes beyond nobility. Jim and Penny Caldwell, your discoveries are amazing. Alton Ganksy, Jon Farrar, Mary Keeley, Linda Schlafer, Dave Lindstedt, and everyone at Tyndale who had a part, your contributions and directions made all this possible.

Robert Cornuke

Foreword

The Exodus of the Hebrew nation from Egypt was a hinge in history that changed the world forever. The Ark of the Covenant was the centerpiece of Hebrew worship. In the pages that follow, I will attempt to lift a candle into the dim chambers of ancient history to snatch a glimpse of the Exodus and stand in the shadow of the Ark. This journey will undoubtedly step on some sacred and scholarly traditions, and what I found along the way may provoke some strong reactions. It is not my intent to disprove anyone's long-held beliefs, but rather to illuminate hidden truths that have been awaiting discovery all along.

PART 1
The Quest for the Mountain of Fire

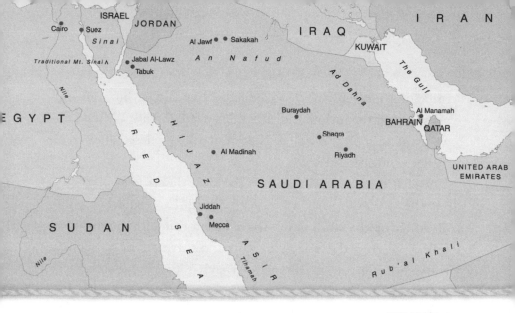

Saudi Arabia, 1988

As each hour passed, we had less water, and with each mile, less gas. Worse yet, it appeared we were straying even farther into the blistering Saudi Arabian desert. We desperately needed to find the paved road that cut across the northwest Saudi frontier. That illusive vein of highway would lead us the hundred or so miles back to Tabuk, to a hotel with clear, cool water and air-conditioning. I tried to drive the pickup onto a rise where I could get my bearings, but the two-wheel-drive Datsun couldn't negotiate the steep slope.

I slammed my boot on the gas pedal as if stomping harder would somehow give us traction. The threadbare tires spun without biting into the loose rock. I offered Larry, my traveling companion, a weak smile. His face was caked in grimy sweat, and I could only imagine what I looked like. Larry said nothing. He simply stared at the incline and shook his head. Finally, I leaned forward and shut off the engine. The Saudi Arabian desert showed no mercy to novices like us.

We left the truck and stood on the loose desert soil.

"This worn-out truck will never make it," Larry said, beginning to trudge up the sandy draw. There was nothing for me to do but follow. We crested the ridge together and surveyed the horizon. In every direction we saw desolate stretches of sand, bleak rocky bluffs, and high, barren mountains.

I pulled a topographical map from my shirt pocket and carefully unfolded it. I studied its contours for a long minute and surveyed distant geographical landmarks. "I know where we are," I said.

"Really? Where?" Larry asked, craning his neck to see our position.

I wadded the map into a ball and proclaimed, "Lost, that's where we are—lost."

Far to the east, I saw the movement of wild camels. Beyond them, a small truck generated a billowing dust spout. The truck was headed our way.

"There!" I shouted, my voice raspy and parched.

Larry looked east and saw the welcome apparition. We trotted down the sloping wadi to our truck. I started the engine and jammed the gears into reverse. Cranking the wheel and gunning the engine, I hightailed it in the general direction of the rising dust cloud. The battered vehicle bounced along the rocky grade as we careened down to the thin, rutted wisp of a road. We soon met the approaching truck, which slowed immediately. Pulling alongside, we could see the driver, a nervous-looking Bedouin who peered warily into our truck. He sat back with his arm resting on the window ledge and waited for us to speak.

I leaned out the window and blurted out, "Asphalt." I had heard other Bedouins use this term to describe the paved highway. The startled driver became even more baffled when Larry leaned across my side of the truck and used awkward hand gestures to communicate our dire need to find the blacktop road. For several anxious moments, the man pondered our plight. Dropping his arm from the window, he surveyed our beleaguered truck, scarred and dusty from its pilgrimage across the desert. His dark eyes seemed to brighten with understanding. Putting his truck in gear, he waved for us to follow and vanished in a fresh cloud of dust.

I whipped our truck around, steering a tight arc to avoid straying off the hard-packed grooves into shifting sand. I had already had enough of getting stuck to last a lifetime.

We followed the Bedouin across mile after mile of wasteland, through a broad canyon to an outpost in the middle of nowhere, nothing more than a few black wool tents and three mud hovels stuck onto the chalky cliffs. Two large, rusted water tanks, supported by a leaning wooden platform, were the only landmarks. Some words were painted in block print on one of the weathered wood planks, but sandblasting windstorms had long since rendered the lettering illegible.

As I stepped from the truck, a gust of hot wind swept sand into my face and pelted my sunglasses with grit. Bedouin men in drab robes squatted in the meager shade of the two tanks, seemingly uninterested in our arrival. The whole village had an otherworldly feel to it. Apparently, people came here from miles around to fill their tanks with gas, get water, and conduct their desert trade.

"Uh-oh," Larry whispered. "This doesn't look good."

I turned to see six men walking toward us, brandishing battered rifles. I was shaken by the unmistakable anger in their eyes. These desert dwellers wore flowing Bedouin robes stained yellow by the harsh sun. I guessed that they were some of the frontier forces I had heard about, a kind of desert police who handled feuds and disputes between remote Bedouin clans. They had now caught two Americans wandering in the desert near a fenced military facility.

Larry and I were quickly surrounded and escorted to one of the huts. Patches of whitewash peeled from its crumbling daub walls. A rifle butt prodded us along until we stood before the hut's darkened doorway. I instinctively stopped short, but a foot against my lower back propelled me inside. Turning in anger, I could make out only the outline of a man standing in the entryway, his robed frame eclipsing the blinding rays of the sun. As my eyes adjusted to the darkness, I heard the word *Jew* and felt warm spittle trickle down my cheek.

We were pushed to the ground inside the hut and awaited the worst.

A stocky man in frayed military fatigues pushed past the other guards and tossed a camel saddle on the floor. Dust rose in the stifling air of the dimly lit room. With an exaggerated huff, the man lowered himself onto the saddle and glared at me from a brutish, sun-scarred face like blistered leather. One eye, blood red and puffy, was swollen nearly shut, but the appraising stare of his good eye was unnerving.

Larry and I sat on the packed-earth floor, our backs pressed against a sweat-stained wall. Our socks, shoes, keys, wallets, and passports had been confiscated and piled in the middle of the room. The rusted tin roof radiated triple-digit heat as thin shafts of sunlight pierced through random gaps and holes, further irritating my sunburnt skin. I lowered my head and waited for the questioning to begin—angry words shouted in a language I didn't understand. My answers—and Larry's—were equally incomprehensible to our captors.

A whipping wind whistled around the mud walls, blowing sand through the cracks and under the door. The air in the room was nauseating. An odor of putrefied mutton oozed from the floor and walls; it clung to my skin, invaded my nose, and mingled with my sweat-saturated hair. I had been fighting my stomach from the moment they had shoved us into this wretched place. I kept my breath shallow and rhythmic, battling the urge to retch.

Our Bedouin guards started in on us again, grilling us incessantly with unintelligible, mind-numbing questions. Although no one understood a word we said, they kept the interrogation going. The one word that I did understand chilled my blood. The men kept calling us Jews with vehement hatred. I studied the guards more closely. Their flowing, sun-faded *thobes* were stained with gun grease and dried sheep's blood. Strapped across their chests were stiff, cracked-leather bandoliers filled with bullet casings of various sizes though most were either empty or corroded. Traditional red-checkered *gutra* scarves were wrapped around their heads and secured with rope headbands. They looked like extras from *Lawrence of Arabia*.

I glanced at Larry, but no conversation was needed. We were in deep trouble, and we both knew it. This was not a place of constitutional liberties for tourists gone astray; there would be no Miranda rights or attorney visits. Our next stop could well be the bottom of a shallow, sandy grave—if they bothered to bury us at all. We were in forbidden territory in a culture closed to the outside world. We were trespassers, and the punishment for this offense could be severe.

We had come in pursuit of a great historical prize so alluring that we had decided to risk everything, but at the moment, I questioned our wisdom.

What made me think this trip was such a good idea? I had left my family at home, set aside my business—and for what? Was it really worth the danger, the pain, the risk? Was it really worth *this*?

I looked away from my red-eyed inquisitor and gazed through a crack in the wall. The sun was dissolving, silhouetting a solitary Bedouin shepherd against the deep blue of the darkening sky. At his feet, a small flock of sheep foraged for scant offerings of desert sage. Although I couldn't see it from where I sat, I knew that the blackened summit of Jabal al-Lawz, "Mountain of the Almond," towered above the distant range of brooding mountains. It held a mysterious relic of antiquity, an age-old secret. Just the night before, Larry and I had stood on that mountain, and what we had seen would change Bible maps and our own lives forever. Now all we had to do was live to tell the story.

For me, that story had begun ten years earlier on a quiet spring evening in Southern California when I answered a call on my police radio.

Southern California, 1978

"All 44 units," the dispatcher's voice crackled over the radio, "we have a truck on fire on Continental Avenue—suspicious circumstances."

I was a crime scene investigator for the Costa Mesa Police Department, a plainclothesman driving an unmarked car. I was right around the corner from Continental Avenue, so I radioed back "910," meaning that I'd take the call.

When I arrived at the scene, a ball of flames and thick black smoke engulfed a charred truck in someone's front yard. In the dying light of dusk, the bright orange glow illuminated a man standing behind the front screen door of the house.

I approached cautiously, and as I neared the porch, I could see a bottle in the man's left hand. I took a few more steps toward the house—and froze. I was staring into the barrel of a semiautomatic rifle pointed squarely at my head. I wanted to reach under my sports jacket for my 9 mm handgun but thought better of it and backed off.

"You a cop?" the man demanded from the doorway. His speech was slurred.

"Uh, no," I managed.

The man pressed the barrel against the screen, making it bulge, "Then get out of here!"

I slowly backed away. A moment later I heard a loud crack overhead, followed by another. Leaves from a nearby tree rained down on me as bullets ripped through its branches. I'm not sure why the man started shooting. Maybe he had seen the yellow light mounted in the rear window of my unmarked police vehicle, which I had parked directly in front of his house. As I dove behind the car, bullets peppered the ground behind me, kicking up a spray of asphalt against my pant legs. I was pinned down with nowhere to go. Backup officers soon arrived, but the standoff with the gunman would drag on for hours.

As night fell, the truck fire burned itself out, leaving smoldering rubber that filled the air with a noxious pall of lingering smoke. A thin fog began to creep in from the coast. The darkness had long since swallowed the man inside the house.

After an eternity of silence, the waiting suddenly ended as the man kicked open the screen door and advanced in my direction. He staggered past the burned-out hull of his pickup truck, spewing random shots from the rifle on his hip.

A sour film of adrenaline crawled across my tongue. Sweat trickled down my back as I lifted my 12-gauge shotgun over the hood of the car and took aim. As I squeezed the trigger, I heard a loud report from another officer's weapon just to my right. Then the 12-gauge erupted in my hand, and the muzzle flash blinded me as I hunched back down behind the protection of my vehicle.

All was quiet again. When I peered back over the hood, I could see the gunman lying on the ground with the rifle at his feet. I inched my way toward him, my grip tight on the shotgun and my hands moist with sweat. I could hear the sucking sound of the man's chest wounds.

When I reached his side, my heart was pounding wildly, but the death rattle had ceased, and the man was clearly gone.

Later, I learned that the burning truck had been a trap to lure a police officer to the scene so that the man could shoot him. Had I not been in plain clothes, that officer might have been me. A recent arrest, the loss of his job, and other pressures of life had pushed the man beyond his limits. In his alcohol-clouded mind, the cops were to blame. He had decided that life wasn't worth living, but before he left this world, he wanted to even the score by snuffing a cop.

I acted as if it didn't bother me—that's what policemen do. But the image of a dying man isn't easy to forget. I soon realized that this moment required me to reassess my life.

I began my law enforcement career as an energetic young police officer, ready for excitement and the opportunity to help others. I worked on patrol, had several special assignments, was a motorcycle cop, and was assigned to the SWAT team. Eventually, I became a crime scene investigator, finding and collecting evidence.

Police work runs hot and cold; it alternates between yawning boredom and adrenaline-charged excitement in the blink of an eye. The job takes a great emotional and physical toll, and after years of this, many experienced cops opt for another profession. I was one of them.

Maybe the shooting was the final straw, or perhaps it was all the death I had encountered as an investigator, but mostly I saw the disillusionment of many older officers who had endured a lifetime of stress, death, crime, and fear. Some were burned-out shells, straining unhappily for the finish line of retirement.

Was that what I had to look forward to?

I wanted something more out of life—but I wasn't sure what. I had no idea that my quest would one day lead me halfway around the world to risk my life in the forbidding sands of the Middle East, searching for lost relics and evidence of an ancient journey.

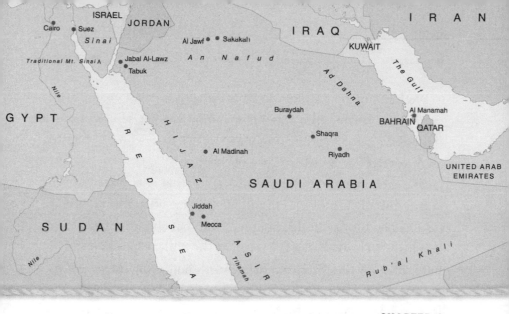

Colorado Springs, 1985

It's a long way from the smoggy southland of California to the crisp mountain air of Colorado, in distance and in every other way. Within months of the shooting, I had resigned from the police force, moved to Colorado, and begun selling real estate with my brother. We eventually started our own company, and together we built a thriving business. Paul was a great partner, and those were some good years.

It was serene living in the mountains. There were no sirens, only wind rustling in the pines. Life was peaceful, stable, predictable, and safe—almost too safe. That was my life on the day I met former astronaut Jim Irwin, the eighth man to walk on the moon. We were introduced by a mutual friend who thought Jim might want to meet me.

We had lunch in Colorado Springs with a small group of his family and friends. Jim was his customary quiet self, without a trace of the arrogance one might expect in a man who had planted an American flag on the surface of the moon.

The table banter spun around the weather, gas prices, sports, and eventually Jim's space flight. He told me about an experience he'd had on his Apollo 15 lunar mission that changed him forever and inspired his belief in the truth of the Bible. While standing in lunar dust on the threshold of infinity and gazing into the darkness of eternal space, something had stirred deep in his soul. He had raised the visor on his helmet and slowly turned to look back at Earth. It was as tiny and fragile as a Christmas tree ornament. Green, brown, white, and blue, this warm, living orb was suspended in the cold vacuum of space. At that moment, Jim said, he knew that God was the master designer and creator of it all.

After returning to Earth, Jim felt that it was time to leave NASA and begin the adventure of a new goal beyond the moon, of seeking evidence for events depicted in the Bible, including the remains of Noah's ark. I was fascinated by his quest, though I didn't know what to make of a famous astronaut's risking ridicule in search of a relic that many people thought was nothing more than myth or legend.

After lunch, Jim turned to me and said, "I hear you were a policeman—a SWAT team member—and that you have been shot at and had to shoot back. I also hear you were trained to handle hostile situations."

"Uh, yeah," I answered awkwardly, wondering why he was interested in my past.

"Someday I might need someone like you to go with me to the

eastern frontier of Turkey. That country has been in ethnic tur-moil, with Kurds fighting against Turks in a bloody civil war that has gone on for generations." The Kurds, Jim cautioned, would want to capture him, hoping to bring worldwide attention to their cause. He paused a second, then said, "I would want a guy like you along, just in case."

❦

When Jim and I met again several months later, he asked if I would go with him to Turkey to look for Noah's ark. I jumped at the chance. Who wouldn't want to travel to distant lands with a for-mer Apollo astronaut? It was a thrilling prospect. As for the risk, I had known plenty of it as a policeman, so my instant enthusiasm didn't surprise me. My life had become somewhat tame, and here was a chance to get a taste of adventure again. Still, I wasn't con-vinced that there was anything to find.

I explained to Jim that I believed in God and Jesus, but my faith didn't quite extend to Noah and the Flood. I cringed, thinking that my disclosure of doubt would eliminate me from being on his team, but Jim said resolutely, "That's why it's so important that we try to find the ark. Finding it will help many like you who are strug-gling in their faith."

I nodded in agreement, but I still wasn't sure what to think. Back then, I went to church once in a while, mostly from a sense of obligation. I wasn't passionate about the Bible—unlike my former partner on the police force, Sig Swanstrom. When we were young cops together, Sig was the one who introduced me to the teachings of the Bible. I had grown up in a household devoid of spiritual guidance. My father was a bartender, and we never attended church as a family. When I went to college, my professors told me that church was an archaic institution and that faith belonged to the intellectually inferior. I bought their logic, as did most of my friends.

Sig, on the other hand, was the son of a history professor at a Christian university, and he accepted the Bible with a certainty I had never seen before. I was a wisecracking skeptic who taunted him mercilessly about his faith, but Sig endured my deprecating comments, and in spite of my satirical portrayal of his beliefs, we became the best of friends and still are.

One evening at the end of our shift, Sig stopped me in the hallway and held up an evidence bag. "This has a knife in it that was left at the scene by a robber who got away," he said. "This knife is sort of like the Bible, Bob." I looked at him oddly, but I was used to Sig's drawing faith illustrations from common elements of life and work. He said, "If we can find fingerprints on this knife that match a suspect's prints, then this knife becomes a very powerful piece of evidence that could send that man to prison. But if we don't even look for those prints, or if we fail to see them, even if they are right there in front of us, then this knife is only a twelve-dollar piece of plastic and steel." He paused for a moment to let that sink in. "Bob, if you fail to look at the Bible, you will never see the fingerprints of God on its pages, and the most powerful written source in the universe will be nothing more to you than a twelve-dollar book made of ink, paper, and glue."

With Sig's encouragement, I finally took a closer look at the evidence, and in time I came to believe in the truth about God and Jesus. But accepting Jesus was a far cry from a wholesale belief in the Bible. All those accounts of spectacular miracles in the Old Testament were a stretch for me. The stories from Genesis and Exodus were a confusing jumble of animal sacrifices, plagues, pillars of fire, a worldwide flood, and other such legends. I knew I wasn't alone in my doubts. A broad philosophical schism exists between scholars who accept the Bible totally and those who have great difficulty in accepting miraculous claims at face value. I was content to go to church and stay in the safe boat with Jesus—but not in the boat with Noah during the Flood.

When Sig was sharing his colorful illustrations with me, I knew he wasn't trying to shove his faith down my skeptical throat. He was just a concerned friend asking me to take a look at the evidence. Now a distinguished astronaut was asking me to do the same thing. Jim Irwin was inviting me to go with him to search for timbers from an old boat. If we found them, they would build a bridge across the chasm of my unbelief.

~

Jim called me again a short time later to suggest that I start getting in top physical condition by running and climbing some of Colorado's "Fourteeners"—the 14,000-foot peaks found throughout the Rocky Mountains. I took the suggestion to heart. The following morning I headed out for a brisk run on a dirt road that snaked up a hill from my house. The sky was an azure blue; the pines gave off the sweet aroma of rising sap, and I made it about two hundred yards before I doubled over, gasping for air. I felt like I was breathing through a soda straw.

What have I gotten myself into? I wondered as I limped home. Little did I know how often I would ask myself that same question over the next twenty years as my quest for adventure and knowledge led me to places I never thought I would go.

The next day my feet were pounding that same mountain road, and I made it a quarter of a mile. The day after that, I ran a half mile, and within a month I hit the five-mile mark. But even as I began to work myself into shape, I realized that I didn't know the first thing about climbing a mountain, and neither did any of my business buddies. The only way any of them would be found standing on a 14,000-foot mountain peak would be as survivors of a plane crash. I recruited the help of two experienced climbers, free-spirited guys from a neighboring town. Off we went to the nearby Rockies, carting an assortment of pitons, ice axes, ropes, and carabiners. We climbed Pike's Peak in a snowstorm, and a few weeks later we trudged through waist-deep snow to the top of Mount Quandary.

As I climbed those majestic mountain peaks, I began to think about what had happened to Jim Irwin on the moon. Standing at the top of those icy summits, I saw the awesome panorama of creation around me, and I felt close to God. I even imagined myself climbing 17,000-foot Mount Ararat in a blinding snowstorm and, my heart pounding like a drum, stumbling across decaying timbers from Noah's ark. I could see it all in my mind—I would scale an icy cliff and peer down into a canyon, where the ominous dark outline of the ark would be barely visible through the distorted optics of ancient ice. It would be the biggest discovery in history, and I would make it.

It didn't happen that way—at least not in 1986. Instead, we were arrested as spies shortly after arriving in Erzurum, a small Turkish town at the base of Mount Ararat. Our capture became worldwide news, with newspaper headlines such as "Astronaut James Irwin Arrested in Turkey: Famous American and Team of Climbers Suspected of Spying."

We had the proper permits. We even had permission to fly an airplane around the mountain. In fact, members of our team had already flown a successful mission around Mount Ararat in a Cessna 206. But that's when the trouble started. When our pilot landed at the airport, the Turkish secret police intercepted our whole team. They accused us of violating airspace over Russia and Iran, an alleged infraction that earned us a rude escort back to our hotel, where armed guards held us under house arrest. As we were being questioned, I couldn't get the prison scenes from the movie *Midnight Express* out of my mind. But that's a story for another time.

As we boarded the plane back to the United States after being released by the Turkish officials, I thought I was finished with international explorations, forbidden lands, nerve-racking arrests, and legends of lost relics.

Little did I know that this ordeal was only the beginning.

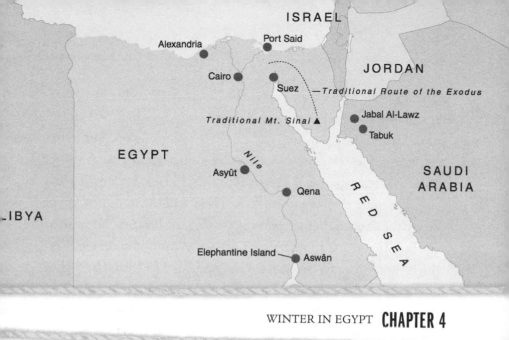

Sinai Peninsula, 1988

The bus belched diesel smoke into a cloudy Egyptian sky as it rumbled down the road across the Nile Delta. We bounced and jolted our way south through a lush landscape that painted a colorful contrast to the waterless sand stretching out from the edges of the world-famous river delta. Channels of life-giving water snaked through miles of rich farmland. Vast fields of cotton, maize, and rice carpeted the terrain. Water buffalo worked the plows, turned wheels to grind grain, or grazed in lazy indifference. Rows of soldier-straight palm trees stood along the roads. In the irrigation streams, rustic paddle wheels engaged the steadily flowing current in an endless dance.

Once again I was traveling with Jim Irwin toward the middle of nowhere. This time nowhere was the Egyptian Sinai Peninsula. After our thwarted adventure in Turkey two years before, I didn't think I would ever join one of Jim's expeditions again. But here I was, with a research team and a film crew, on a hot bus rambling its way into a vast expanse of desert. This time Jim was bent on discovering the route that the ancient Israelites had taken out of Egypt during the Exodus on their way to crossing the Red Sea. He wanted to follow that route to find the mysterious "Mountain of God" on which—according to the Bible—God appeared to Moses and gave him the Ten Commandments. The ancient text said that Moses encountered God on a remote desert mountain called Mount Sinai. Could the Bible be believed . . . literally? Jim Irwin and the others in our group certainly believed it could. They wanted to experience the place where God had spoken to Moses and had shown his fiery brilliance to the Israelites. They also wanted to determine whether the Egyptian Mount Sinai was the mountain designated in the Bible and collect any evidence they could find of the extraordinary things that had occurred there.

I was still along mostly for the adventure, but this time I found myself wanting—almost needing—to find proof that would satisfy my skeptical heart and mind.

In preparation for the trip, I had read and reread the biblical account of Moses and the Israelites. I was familiar with the story of how Moses was drawn to a burning bush in the desert near Mount Sinai and how God spoke to him there and sent him back to Egypt to lead an entire nation of Hebrew slaves out of bondage to worship God on that same mountain. The Israelites camped near the foot of Mount Sinai while Moses went up the mountain to receive the Ten Commandments from God.

The exact route taken by Moses and the people of Israel is unknown. No one has ever pulled signs from the sands of Egypt that point the way to the Exodus event. No trace of evidence has been unearthed that suggests that the traditional Mount Sinai in Egypt—a major tourist destination—is the holy mountain spoken of in the Bible. Most people who visit the traditional site on the Sinai Peninsula are unaware that the mountain they see is only one of several sites proposed as the real Mount Sinai. I had heard that Helena, the mother of Constantine, emperor of Rome in the third century, first christened this mountain in the Sinai Peninsula as the location of Mount Sinai. After her declaration, the mountain quickly became a pilgrimage site and was thus designated on maps of the region. This tradition, however, is unproven, and support for Helena's claim is murky at best. I hoped that we would be able to determine whether or not this was the right mountain.

I had always imagined the Exodus from Egypt as a long, hot journey through scorching desert sands. No doubt Moses and the people encountered plenty of arid terrain and searing heat, but I realized that it wasn't all like that as I stepped off the bus into a midwinter blast of cold air. Bruised gray clouds piled up in the sky, swallowing the craggy peak of the Egyptian Mount Sinai. We craned our necks to catch a glimpse of the famous mountain. Like the weather, it wasn't what I expected.

The next day, with Jim and others in our group, I would climb the craggy slopes like so many pilgrims before me. Like them, I would wonder if I was tracing Moses' steps. But tonight I was looking forward to a good night's sleep in a warm bed. I chastised myself for bringing only a light sweater. As we gathered our luggage outside the hotel, it began to snow, putting an exclamation point on my inadequate choice of clothing.

Snow in Egypt. In hindsight, it made sense. We were 5,000 feet above sea level, plenty high enough for snow. With the other twelve team members, I moved quickly to the hotel lobby, ready for a warm meal, a warm room, and a warm bed. Unfortunately, there had been a mix-up in the reservations, and not enough rooms were available to accommodate our entire group. After searching other nearby hotels, rooms were found for everyone but me. Our group had already doubled and tripled up. There wasn't even a couch or a cot to be had. The hotel clerk, clearly embarrassed, suggested that I try a "very economical inn" at the end of the road. As dusk turned to dark, I lugged my duffel bag through the biting wind and sleet to a dilapidated stone building. Inside, the rooms had pieces of plywood on stacks of bricks for beds and a hole in the floor as bathroom facilities. A plastic sheet with a faded pink floral print was stapled onto the plywood—a nice designer touch, I thought. The room reminded me of a butcher's walk-in freezer. I wanted to go back to the hotel and beg for a place to sleep on the floor, but I was afraid the other guys might think I was a wimp. So instead I said, "Hey, what's one night and a little bit of cold?"

There were no towels, sheets, or blankets, only that ugly, cold plastic sheet stapled to the unforgiving plywood and a roll of toilet paper on the floor. Removing everything from my duffel bag, I made a nest of my clothing and settled down in the middle, pulling everything around me like a gerbil in sawdust. I unrolled the toilet paper and piled T-shirts, dirty towels, used underwear, smelly socks—even magazines and open books—over myself from head to toe to keep from freezing. The only heat source was a single dim bulb above the door. Outside my room, a drunken band of Egyptian men sang into the night, warmed by a roaring fire as they broke bottles, laughed, and shot their rifles into the air.

It was not the best night I ever spent. I couldn't sleep. The howling wind blew icy gusts under the door and through gaps in the windows. I felt like a prisoner in Siberia. The good news was that the room only cost me two dollars.

Morning brought a clear sky with only a few scrappy clouds. Through the window of my monastic accommodations, I could see Mount Sinai awash in the brilliant morning sunlight. I bundled my things and walked outside. Tourists snapped pictures of Mount Sinai, which glistened with a dusting of snow. The rising sun melted the snow into rivulets of water that the thirsty ground immediately consumed.

Dawn also brought to light the full scope of the tourist trade that had grown up around the mountain. Roadside merchants hawked trinkets, candy, and religious mementos. It was a gaudy, troubling sight.

I shouldered my duffel bag and walked up a road beyond the merchants to the famous Saint Catherine's Monastery. The team was already gathered by a large cypress tree. Jim Irwin was chatting with an elderly monk dressed in traditional Orthodox garb. I tossed my bag inside the bus.

"What's Jim doing?" I asked a team member.

"Trying to arrange a tour of the Skull House."

The Skull House is formally known as the Chapel of Saint Triphone. It earned its popular name from a macabre collection kept by the monks.

Following the group inside, I saw a large, neatly arranged pile of human skulls kept in place by a chicken-wire fence. Skulls were stacked so high that some had rolled off like apples from a produce display. The room had the musty, catacomb smell of decaying bones that dated to the fourth century. The elderly monk raised his hand in protest when a team member started taking a picture of the morbid sight.

The monk offered an apologetic grin. "Don't be concerned. These are the bones of the monks who have died here at Saint Catherine's Monastery since its construction under order of Emperor Justinian from 527 to 565. When a monk dies, we bury him in our courtyard cemetery. Because space is limited, we dig up the body three months later and put the bones in here."

"But why?" someone asked.

"It is our tradition. The bones are a constant symbol of our temporal existence, reminding us of our insignificance here at the foot of Mount Sinai. We know our bones will be thrown on that pile with the others. It helps us keep our eyes off ourselves and on God."

In the middle of the knobby pile of skulls was a full skeleton, propped in the high-backed chair of a potentate and attired in a moth-eaten velvet robe. *One of the former abbots,* I surmised. Of the hundreds of skeletons in that room, each no doubt represented a devout man. All who had served here believed that this monastery stood on holy ground, near the mountain where Moses met with God. Our eyes lingered on the pile of skulls as the old monk shuffled past almost unnoticed. He led us back out into the sunlight where Mount Sinai towered in the distance.

Jim Irwin was eager to start climbing the mountain, and he asked if I would hike with him to the top. Together we trekked up the mountainside, following old steps carved centuries earlier by monks. Along the path, we saw a rusted sign saying Moses' Mountain.

Jim never stopped to rest. He plugged along like a machine—not fast but always persevering, in keeping with his personality. Jim was persistent about everything. Many years before, he had been in a plane crash that had left him with a compound break in his ankle, two broken legs, and a fractured jaw. Doctors wanted to amputate his foot and informed him that he would never walk again. Jim Irwin had a different opinion. He not only walked again, but he walked on the moon!

When we crested the 7,500-foot mountain, Jim wasn't even breathing hard. I, on the other hand, had to bend over to catch my breath because Jim's unrelenting pace had taken its toll. We spent the next thirty minutes scrutinizing the mountain's crags and outcroppings, scouting its hidden walls and gullies. We looked for specific features such as geologic obelisks, peculiar terrain, or man-made imprints that would suggest that the Israelites had gathered here as described in the book of Exodus. There was nothing. Scanning the horizon, we saw only jagged mountain peaks.

Jim asked a pointed question: "If this is Mount Sinai, then why aren't we on the backside of a desert as the Bible says?"

From my study of the book of Exodus, I knew that he was referring to the first verse of the third chapter: "Now Moses was tending the flock of Jethro his father-in-law, the priest of Midian, and he went deep into the wilderness near Sinai, the mountain of God."

Jim was right. Nothing that should be here was here. Jim had begun with the assumption that the accounts of Moses and Mount Sinai were accurately portrayed in the Bible. Study of those ancient accounts had led him to expect certain proofs to be present: the cave of Moses, tribe markers, altars, running water, and other confirmations that we were standing on the true Mount Sinai. But what was supposed to be here wasn't.

The Bible says that the Israelites lived at the foot of Mount Sinai for almost a year. They built several altars and conducted many ceremonies there. God performed miracles at the mountain, including a fiery display at its peak. A rock was split, and water gushed from the fissure. Even after three thousand years, there should be some evidence of these events. But teams of archaeologists have scoured the traditional Mount Sinai and have found nothing. Not a bone, clay pot, or miniscule fragment could be linked in any way to the Exodus.

Because of this, many archeologists have dismissed the great Exodus altogether. Jim had come to believe that the problem was not with the biblical story but with the assumed location of Mount Sinai. As I stood atop the mountain touted for centuries as the most important peak in history, I came to the same conclusion (as have many scholars before me): Saint Catherine's Monastery is not on the real Mount Sinai. Visiting the site had proved the point for me.

There was a degree of sadness to all of this. I couldn't help thinking of the monks whose bones were kept in the stone building at the foot of the mountain, of the tourists who had come to see a holy place, and of those who would continue to come.

When we reached the bottom of the mountain, camel drivers still vied for passengers, and vendors still hawked their garish trinkets from squalid stands. The powerful stench of animal and human waste insulted my nostrils. Jim looked at me and said, "This is ridiculous. There is no way this is Mount Sinai."

These were not casual words uttered after a few moments' thought. I reminded myself that the speaker was the first astronaut to explore both the Hadley Rille and the Apennie Mountains of the moon. Jim Irwin was a master navigator, expert surveyor, world-class explorer, and trained scientist. The lunar module pilot of Apollo 15 was telling me, "Bob, this ain't it."

I had to agree. But if this mountain at the southern end of the Sinai Peninsula wasn't it, then what was? I intently scanned the mountains on the horizon. . . . Did such a mountain exist? I knew that Jim and the others in our group would have some ideas and that we would be talking late into the night.

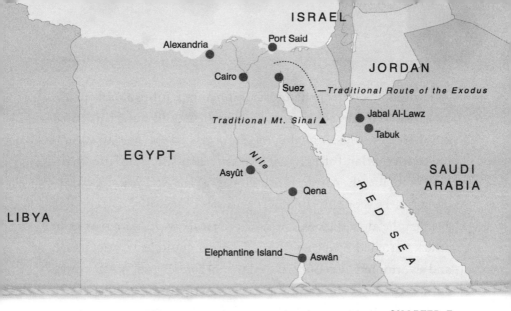

ISRAEL

Alexandria Port Said

JORDAN

Cairo

Suez *—Traditional Route of the Exodus*

Traditional Mt. Sinai ▲ Jabal Al-Lawz

Tabuk

EGYPT

Asyût *Nile*

Qena R E D   S E A

SAUDI
ARABIA

LIBYA

Elephantine Island — Aswân

TO THE TIP OF SINAI **CHAPTER 5**

Within the hour, we were on the bus headed southwest toward the southern tip of the Sinai Peninsula to explore a new theory, an idea so revolutionary that it could shatter sixteen hundred years of paradigms.

With the traditional Mount Sinai disappearing behind us, we left hundreds of years of entrenched belief behind in our rearview mirror. The bus bounced down a long, twisting road out of the high, craggy mountains. A generous sun provided a welcome day of warmth. After a sleepless night in a freezing room, I appreciated this more than most. I lowered a window and let the balmy desert air blow over my face. Outside, a forsaken stretch of chiseled canyons and sandy draws rolled by, revealing a stark desert panorama. I saw no tents or even a single sheep on the sand-choked plains and jutting hills.

The Sinai is one of the most uninhabited, inhospitable places on earth. I couldn't imagine why anyone would want this place, but there were those who did. In 1967 a fast-paced, six-day war was waged for this land after Egypt blockaded key shipping lanes in the Gulf of Aqaba, the easternmost "finger" of the Red Sea, thus strangling Israel's economic lifeline. Centuries of hostility had come to a violent head, and Israel was quick to retaliate. Its devastating air attack flattened Egypt's air force before it could leave the tarmac, and an armored tank blitz routed the Jordanian and Syrian armies at their borders. This military masterstroke won Israel possession of the Sinai Peninsula as a short-lived buffer from her sworn enemies. Israel returned the peninsula to Egypt in 1973, initiating an uneasy truce.

The bus came to a sudden, screeching halt before a man in army fatigues, who held a machine gun at the ready. He was a United Nations checkpoint guard, one of a handful established to monitor the peace agreements resulting from the Six-Day War. We piled out to stretch in this remote alkaline patch of sun-bleached sand while the guard checked everything out. If I was headed nowhere, I felt that I had arrived.

Dr. Roy Knuteson, the leader of our team, walked to the rear of the bus and paused in the afternoon sun. Gazing toward the distant mountains we had just left, he put his hands on the small of his back and bent backward. The good doctor was our resident scholar. He had a distinguished, no-nonsense presence, with his wavy silver hair always impeccably combed and his shirts starched and pressed without a wrinkle even in this sweltering desert. He was one of the reasons we had traveled halfway around the world.

Dr. Knuteson had taken his Exodus research a step further than most. He steadfastly refused to acquiesce to secular interpretations. After his exhaustive study of all available literature on the subject, he still fell short of pinpointing the true Red Sea crossing, so he decided to try a fresh tactic: he dared to examine what Scripture had to say. By taking a hard look at the book of Exodus, he systematically eliminated all known Exodus route theories. He then scoured hundreds of miles of coastline until he identified a tiny stretch of beach at Sharm al-Sheikh on the Gulf of Aqaba, the place where he believed the Red Sea had parted so that the children of Israel could cross out of Egypt.

According to the biblical account, God led the Israelites with a pillar of cloud by day and fire by night to Mount Sinai—a mountain that Dr. Knuteson proposed was across the Gulf of Aqaba to the east of the Sinai Peninsula, in present-day Saudi Arabia. He quoted the apostle Paul from the New Testament: "And now Jerusalem is just like Mount Sinai in Arabia, because she and her children live in slavery" (Galatians 4:25, NLT).

Dr. Knuteson, however, was not the first to propose this theory. In 1936, a man named Stephen L. Caiger commented in his book on biblical archaeology, "A very reasonable conjecture would place the Holy Mount of Sinai, or Horeb, not in the Peninsula, but east of the Gulf of Aqaba in the volcanic region of northern Arabia."[1]

These men—Jim Irwin, Dr. Knuteson, and Stephen Caiger—had me thinking. They took the Bible as a literal, not mythical, representation of history. They believed, as do many others, that the Bible can be trusted as a reliable source for past events. When I stood on the traditional site of Mount Sinai, I used the same criteria to dismiss it as the actual site. Now I had to decide whether to trust the apostle Paul when he said that Mount Sinai was in Arabia, even though popular opinion says that it is on the Egyptian Sinai Peninsula.

Could the Bible be taken literally?

CHARIOTS

Our destination was the site that Dr. Knuteson believed was the crossing point for Moses and the former slaves who left Egypt, and our sightseeing would take place beneath the waves.

Leaving a final checkpoint, the bus meandered through a series of canyons before reaching the broad shore of the Red Sea. Although the likelihood of finding the remains of Pharaoh's chariots was remote at best, our team was buzzing with excitement. The pristine Gulf of Aqaba displayed its dazzling aqua hues, a sapphire oasis in the stark brown sand. Our team hoped that remnants of those chariots had somehow waited under the sea for us to bring them to light.

I knew how unlikely it would be to find a trace of those ancient vehicles. Egyptian chariots were made of lightweight wood, and marine organisms would make short work of them in saltwater. The only parts of a chariot that might survive for thousands of years would be the sturdy bronze wheel hubs or a few fittings. Perhaps there would be bits of armor worn by the Egyptian charioteers. More than likely, the chariots would have had gold-leaf decorations, but in a thin veneer that would not survive in any quantity. For more than thirty-five hundred years, blowing sands had spread tons of silt over the seafloor. Even if we knew where to look, these chariot parts or bits of armor could be buried under thirty feet of silt and sand.

Still, we had to look.

THE CROSSING SITE

The Bible describes the Exodus route of the fleeing Israelites as heading south from Goshen. The escaping Hebrew slaves lacked the military skills to fight the occupants of the northern areas of the Sinai Peninsula, so God did not lead them north through Philistine country. Instead, he led them south to the Red Sea (Exodus 13:17-18). A reasoned deduction, according to Dr. Knuteson and others, is that the route went down the western edge of the peninsula's wide, hard-packed beach, which extends all the way from the Nile Delta in the north to the southern tip of the Sinai Peninsula. At the tip, the road turns up the eastern flank of the Sinai and stops abruptly at an imposing mountain range, whose sheer peaks jut vertically from the shoreline. When we arrived at Sharm al-Sheikh, we could see for ourselves that the terrain there matched the biblical description.

OUT TO SEA

In the morning, we headed out to sea on a chugging old dive boat called the *Apu Hara*. Jim Irwin and his wife, Mary, sat in the bow enjoying the mild temperature and salty air. They were gazing at a freighter that had come to grief years earlier on a reef about two miles ahead of us. Years of sun and salty sea had turned the ship into a beaten metal corpse. The long reef looked like a giant underwater serpent with prey in its jaws, slowly consuming the rusting hulk.

During his initial investigation, Dr. Knuteson saw this reef on satellite photographs. It clearly extended from the shore at Sharm al-Sheikh, straddling the deep rift between the Gulf of Aqaba and Saudi Arabia. This underwater roadway made an ideal crossing site for the escaping Israelites. The Old Testament prophet Isaiah alludes to it when he says, "Are You not the One who dried up the sea, the waters of the great deep; that made the depths of the sea a road for the redeemed to cross over?" (Isaiah 51:10).

On the boat's aft deck, one of our team members, Charles Garrett, tinkered with our metal-detection equipment. Garrett—short, stocky, and bearded—is a world-class expert on metal-detection devices and the founder of a metal-detector manufacturing company. Pass through any airport security checkpoint, and you will see the Garrett brand name on the equipment.

Larry Williams was also on board, having flown to Sharm al-Sheikh to join the team. Larry is a genius at trading commodities—his investment theories have earned him worldwide acclaim and a very large bank account. He once entered ten thousand dollars in an investors contest and in one year turned it into a million dollars. Bored with moneymaking as an end in itself, he ran for the United States Senate and twice won the Republican nomination in Montana. President Reagan campaigned for him, but Larry narrowly lost both elections.

Next, Larry had become interested in archaeology. Sparked by his childhood ambition of becoming a treasure hunter, Larry obtained old maps about forgotten lost treasure and spent weekends in remote western desert hills, exploring dark caves and shinnying across sheer, rocky ledges, looking for strange markings on cliffs that might lead to the treasure he sought. He found it tantalizing that most archaeological discoveries were not made by prominent, academically pedigreed scholars but by the happenstance dumb luck of amateur treasure hunters. The oldest petroglyphs in America were found in the Grand Canyon by a lonely cowpoke out for a morning ride. A shepherd boy searching for a stray goat found the Dead Sea Scrolls in a cave.

Larry was driven to adventure through the anticipation of pulling a dusty old relic from the desert floor and seeing the glint of gold or of making an archaeological discovery of immense importance. It was the raw thrill of exploring—for adventure rather than monetary gain—that lured him into terrain more hospitable to sharks and scorpions than to millionaires. Now this wealthy benefactor had funded our entire expedition.

The dive team was busy checking regulators, putting on wet suits, and gathering film equipment. Larry and I were the odd men out. It felt awkward not to have diving skills so that we could help. Soon the equipment-laden divers plunged into the sea and disappeared in a swirl of blue bubbles, and all Larry and I could do was sit and wait. After a half hour of doing nothing, Larry got that glimmer in his eye that meant, "Hey, Bob, let's go down and look around."

"We're not certified divers," I said. It wasn't much of a protest.

"It doesn't look difficult. Just breathe in and out real slow and don't stay down too long." I thought there might be more to it than that, but I went along. We ran the idea past the skipper, a forty-something American with long, tangled hair. He was a holdout from the 1960s with a carefree lifestyle to match, who liked to be called "the boat dude."

"No problemo, guys," Boat Dude said. "I'll hook you up with some gear. Just don't stay down more than twenty minutes, don't go down too deep, and don't come up any faster than your rising bubbles."

After this thorough thirty-second training session, we squirmed into our wet suits and had the heavy diving gear cinched on. I felt as if I had an engine block strapped to my back. I would plunge to the bottom like a boulder.

The skipper quickly showed us how to use the buoyancy control, and we popped the hard rubber regulators into our mouths.

"See ya, man," he said as he nudged us backward off the gunwales.

Larry and I hit the water together. I had a moment of panic, but once I realized that I was floating and not dropping like an anchor, I was able to slow my breathing and begin to enjoy the process. Once we had gained the slow, easy rhythm of inhaling and exhaling, we released some air from the buoyancy control and gently descended into the darkening world of liquid wonder.

Seeing the reef underwater brought a surprising new perspective. Its sheer walls rose dramatically from the depths, topping off just a few feet below the surface. Could this be the roadway that the prophet Isaiah spoke of? Had surging walls of water mounted up on each side? I felt a chill that didn't come from the water. Another Bible verse that Jim and the others had discussed came to mind: "With the blast of Your nostrils the waters were gathered together; the floods stood upright like a heap; and the depths congealed in the heart of the sea" (Exodus 15:8).

Our academic reading suddenly came to life as Larry and I swam along the edge of the reef. We stayed down about fifteen minutes, but it seemed like only seconds as we moved along the impressive structure. Schools of fish, like mirrors, reflected the rays of the sun that pierced the surface. The Red Sea abounds with life, only inches from the dead, baked sands of the desert. We surfaced, reentering the familiar world of gravity and air and bringing with us a better understanding of what might have happened almost thirty-five hundred years before.

It was nearly dark when the *Apu Hara* dropped anchor a few

hundred yards offshore from Sharm al-Sheikh. The diving team had found rusted debris from many ships that had run aground on the reef, an assortment of tin cans and engine parts, and a number of indefinable pieces of corroded metal—but no ancient chariot parts. The currents were fierce and the depths too great to bear for long. Pieces of recent wrecks were already under a foot of sand. There was no way to tell what thirty-five hundred years of currents and sand might have done. As the team stowed their gear belowdecks, no one wanted to talk.

I sat topside with Jim and Larry. The moon shone bright, and spindles of light danced like diamonds off the calm waters. Silence gave way to a spirited dialogue about the day's events and the meaning of the reef.

As if talking to himself, Jim Irwin said, "If that's where they passed through the sea, then Mount Sinai has to be ... over there."

He pointed to a distant ribbon of shadowy land, nearly invisible in the darkening mottled sky?—the west coast of Saudi Arabia. Until then, the legendary mountain where Moses received the Ten Commandments had remained in the background of our daily discourse.

"Bob, do you see it?" Jim asked. "Mount Sinai is in Saudi Arabia. The Bible says in Galatians that Mount Sinai is in Arabia. That's where it has to be."

Dr. Knuteson's idea about the land bridge made the idea seem all the more plausible.

In silence, we gazed across the Gulf toward the few twinkling lights dotting the Saudi Arabian coastline. I had stood on the traditional Mount Sinai and found it lacking. I had gazed at a possible land bridge beneath the surface of the Red Sea, and now in the dark of evening, I felt an urge to stand atop another mountain, hidden somewhere in Saudi Arabia, in the ancient biblical land called Midian.

We dove on the big reef for several more days with similar results. On the last day of our stay in Egypt, our team enjoyed a festive debriefing. It had been an arduous two weeks. Everyone was primed to unwind, say their good-byes, have a few laughs, and trade war stories about an eventful, if disappointing, enterprise. There would be no earthshaking discovery of chariot wheels on this trip. We took great satisfaction, however, in knowing that we had drawn a new line in the sand concerning the Exodus route. If nothing else, we had found for ourselves a practical explanation for the Red Sea crossing and the direction of the real Mount Sinai that was as valid as any theory to date. I left feeling good about the expedition, while realizing that the location of the real Mount Sinai remained an unsolved mystery.

As the evening wore on, Jim pulled Larry and me aside. Reaching into his shirt pocket, he removed a crumpled letter he had received shortly before the trip from a fellow named David Fasold. The note detailed a journey that Fasold had taken into Saudi Arabia some years earlier, when he eventually found and scouted a peak called Jabal al-Lawz. He described the mountain as having the marks of the real Mount Sinai. Reading from the letter, Jim described features on the mountain that at the very least indicated that Fasold had found something incredibly interesting.

Unfortunately, as he left the mountain, which sits in the middle of a vast military reservation, Fasold and his companion, Ron Wyatt, were arrested by Saudi police and spent a terrifying week in jail, charged by the king's prosecutor with "robbing Saudi Arabia of its wealth from antiquities." This was a capital offense that could have resulted in a public beheading. Saudi officials finally re-leased the pair, badly shaken and stripped of all their film, video, and notes—the evidence needed to authenticate their find. Fasold and Wyatt had risked their lives and come up empty-handed, though the harsh Saudi response suggested that they had found a significant archaeological site.

Fasold told Jim Irwin that he would never return to Saudi Ara-bia—it was too dangerous. He had written hoping that the famous astronaut would have the stature and the clout to gain official Saudi clearance and mount a legitimate excavation of the peak. Fasold had given it a historic try, and he now wanted to pass the torch to someone else who might be able to get in and—more im-portant—get out with the evidence.

After what we had just been through, the letter lent stunning force to Dr. Knuteson's theory; practically every piece of evidence from Fasold and Wyatt's trip advanced the notion that Mount Si-nai was in Saudi Arabia. Dangling the letter between thumb and forefinger, Jim smiled and raised a hand toward the eastern hori-zon. There, outlined by a vague line of mist scarcely visible in the twilight, lay the Saudi shoreline.

"What did I tell you?" Jim's voice was edgy with expectancy. "That's where we need to go." Jim handed the letter to Larry, who tucked it carefully into his shirt.

I wouldn't realize until later how completely this information had affected me. But from that moment, my mind began to echo a single question: *What is on the other side of that land bridge?* I felt a sense of urgency and suspense—perhaps akin to what Jim felt be-fore his trip to the moon—about what it would be like to find a site of such historic magnitude.

We spoke no more of it that night, but as we returned to the party, my eye caught Larry's gaze. Despite his deadpan expression, I glimpsed that kindred spark of wonder needed to launch two incurable thrill seekers into the mysterious unknown.

We were going. And we'd find the mountain, one way or another. Of that I was certain.

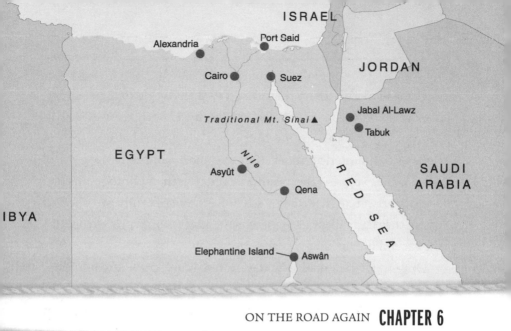

After several months, Larry called. Not given to pleasantries, he got right to the point. "I'm thinking of going to Saudi Arabia very soon to check out the Mount Sinai site. Are you interested in going with me?"

The question caught me off guard. "Am I interested? Of course I'm interested." My mind raced to keep up with my heart as I considered the possibilities.

A few seconds later Larry said, "I'll pay for everything."

Not much to think about there. "Count me in."

"Good. I'll be in touch." He hung up. This short conversation would lead to difficult days and a lifetime of memories.

I thought of the letter that Jim Irwin had given Larry in Egypt. It was not just a wrinkled piece of paper but a map, a guide that pointed to a treasure more valuable than gold. That crumpled note might lead to a discovery that would rock the world of archaeology. It was the chance of a lifetime, and Larry and I both knew it. He had just made it possible for me to follow that dream halfway around the world. I reminded myself that two men had been arrested and jailed while exploring the mountain and that their photographs had been confiscated. They left with no evidence. Could we succeed where they had failed? Perhaps the old adage would prove true: "It's the second mouse that gets the cheese."

Once Larry had made the decision to go, I knew it would happen; he was that kind of a guy. Everything might fall into place, or things could spool apart; it could be easy or difficult, but that didn't matter—Larry would make it happen.

I ran the idea past Jim and learned that he had already talked to Larry. Jim had tried pulling some strings, using his astronaut status to get us into Saudi Arabia, but he had hit a wall. Jim was unaccustomed to hearing "No. You can't come. You're not invited." Out of the 6 billion people on planet Earth, he was one of a dozen who had traveled to the moon. He had been given a ticker-tape parade in New York City. Kings had adjusted their schedules in order to meet him. But apparently no one wanted him in the center of the Saudi kingdom. I could hear the frustration in his voice as he realized that his fame might hinder our chances. He had resigned himself to the fact that he was not going, and disappointment seeped through his words as he said, "Go. Find that mountain."

My next conversation with Larry began with a pointed question: "How are we going to get into the most closed country in the world? The only Americans getting into that country are employed by international oil companies or assigned as military personnel."

Larry said, "Don't worry. We'll get in."

This ambiguous answer meant that he didn't have a clue how we would do it but that somehow we would. In the days ahead, he would spend a pile of money traveling and making countless telephone calls to find a way into Saudi Arabia. Like Jim, he met with failure.

"There is absolutely no way to get a visa into Saudi," he was told.

LONDON

A glimmer of hope surfaced when a friend of Larry's in London said he could get us a visa. Jack Trimonti, a smooth-talking commodities broker, boasted of knowing a Saudi prince who happened to be in London; he assured us that he could get us a sponsorship into Saudi. That fell flat. The prince had flown to Scandinavia to see the northern lights, and we had no idea when he would return. Saudi Arabia again seemed out of reach.

But Jack had not finished. He told Larry to come to London. He had another friend who knew people in high places in the Saudi embassy; this man could get us visas. It was good enough for Larry. He called to say, "It's a go." There was no hesitation in his voice, no wavering. We cleared our calendars and went to London.

Jack, a dapper man with a look of sophistication, met us at the airport. He introduced us to his friend Dimitri, a flamboyant Greek who chain-smoked and spoke in rapid, broken English. He was heavyset; the buttons of his shirt strained to remain in place while threatening to give way at any moment. He struck me as a little shifty, and this image was enhanced by his constant use of the phrase "I assure you there will be no problem." Every time he smiled, I got nervous.

With rock-solid conviction, Dimitri promised that we would have our visas the next day. The next day came, and Dimitri met us with, "Surprising news—no visas." The announcement didn't sit well with Larry, and his displeasure brought a wave of defensiveness from Dimitri. In an effort to save face, he rushed us across town to his office. Rain poured down, making the day as gloomy as our spirits.

Dimitri had an idea. In his files he found an old letter faxed to him from the Saudi prince about an oil deal gone sour. The letter was on royal letterhead and bore the prince's official signature. The logo of the kingdom was at the top. Dimitri programmed his fax machine to match the identification number at the top of the prince's letter and then set it to display the correct time in Saudi Arabia. He did a test fax to a friend. When the friend called to say that the test fax looked like it had come from the royal palace in Saudi Arabia, Dimitri beamed with pride.

"This isn't what I bargained for," I told Larry. I could see what was happening, and I didn't like it. The trip was taking a bad turn. In a matter of days, we had gone from entering the country legally to concocting some wild scheme with a forged royal signature. I'd gone from thinking this was a sure bet to knowing that we were taking our lives in our hands. Dimitri seemed determined to drag us into some grossly illegal intrigue that could get us imprisoned and possibly killed.

My stomach soured as I watched Dimitri make a copy of the letterhead and signature and affix it to the fabricated sponsorship letter. It looked as if the prince had written it, but the signature came off the copier blotchy and blurred. It looked like the fake that it was, and no one knew how to fix it.

I looked at Larry. "I'm very uncomfortable with this. We could get in tremendous trouble." The room went silent except for the splat of raindrops pelting a large window.

"Are you bailing on me, Bob? I've spent a lot of money on this. If you can think of another way, say so now. But I need to know. Are you in?"

There was no other way to get into Saudi Arabia, and I knew it. With those words in my ear, I crossed over. Thousands of miles from home, neck-deep in international intrigue, I felt my manhood was in question, and I bent to the pressure of the moment.

"Yes, I'm in."

Christians are persecuted in Saudi Arabia and more terrorists—including the 9/11 hijackers—have come out of that country than any other. Some might say that this gave me ample justification to maneuver around their laws. Others would say—and with good reason—that it was wrong of me to go into Saudi so covertly. At the time it seemed to be the only choice, a sliver of opportunity dangling in front of us, and we went for it. As the gray clouds turned black, ushering in a dark London evening, I made a fateful choice that I would later regret.

I turned to Dimitri, who sensed my disgust with the whole matter, and demanded the letter with the prince's signature.

"If we're going to do this, let's do it so we don't get caught," I said.

I took the prince's signature and enlarged it on the copier to several times its normal size. I then took a pen and carefully retraced it, coloring in the gaps and imperfections. Then I returned to the copier and reduced the text to normal size. It looked perfect—bold and official. We recopied the letter, transposed it over the prince's signature and letterhead, and faxed it to the Saudi embassy with the preprogrammed Saudi time and country code.

It worked. The embassy faxed us back at a number we had put in the letter, telling us to come down with our papers and passports. With a little more finagling at the Saudi embassy, we were able to make a flight the next day.

Once the door was closed on that Saudi airliner, I knew that there was no turning back. We were exchanging green fields and moderate temperatures for choking dust storms and unimaginable heat. We hoped to find a remote stone sentinel called Jabal al-Lawz, known to the local Bedouins as Jabal Musa—the Mountain of Moses. The adrenaline that had propelled me this far was now waning. The gravity of what we were doing began to settle in my soul.

I had an uneasy feeling about the ruse we had used to gain our visas, but I had come too far to back away now. As Henry Ward Beecher once said, "In things pertaining to enthusiasm, no man is sane who does not know how to be insane on proper occasions." I wondered if this might be a proper occasion for insanity.

JIDDAH

Saudi men and women filled the plane. Most of the men smoked cigarettes, and a noxious blue haze hovered in the cabin. A scratchy recorded prayer to Allah droned over the intercom. People started cramming into the bathrooms to ritually bathe for afternoon prayers. The flight attendants announced the direction of Mecca, and people filled the aisles to kneel and bow toward the heart of Islam, murmuring prayers.

A Saudi man sitting next to me noticed my keen interest in the cultural and religious activity around me. He smiled and asked in perfect English, with only a wisp of Arabic accent, "Why are you going to Saudi Arabia? Are you working for the military? an oil company perchance?"

I stuttered a yes and left it at that.

He smiled and asked nothing further of me but chattered on about himself. He said he was an inventor, an electrical engineer, and went into detail about how Saudis punish criminal offenders by cutting off their hands and sometimes even their heads for transgressions against the laws of the kingdom. He explained that he had invented a new way of amputating hands. He described a laser device that would separate a man's hand from his arm and cauterize the wound at the same time.

"When they use my device, there is very little blood spilled." He seemed very proud. I thought of the forged letter we were carrying and wondered if I was doomed to be this man's first client.

I had had enough of that conversation. Feigning a smile and fluffing my pillow, I turned toward the window and gazed into the high-altitude darkness.

We deplaned at the Jiddah international airport in Saudi Arabia. The night desert air was stifling, unable to slough off the heat of the day. As I left the plane, the heat enveloped me. *What is it like in the broiling daytime sun?* I wondered.

The outside temperature was the least of our problems. Another fire burned inside of me. Ahead of us was a Saudi customs official. The kingdom of Saudi Arabia had unknowingly issued valid travel visas to us two days earlier, based on a letter concocted in a London office. The ramifications of our deceit sent spurts of adrenaline through my body. I could taste it on my tongue.

I got in line behind Larry. An expressionless young man occupied the cubicle before us. When it was Larry's turn, he walked nonchalantly to the customs official and slid his U.S. passport, stamped with the bogus entry visa, across the counter and through a narrow gap below a sheet of protective glass. The young Arab snapped it up. He tapped a few keys on his computer and peered at Larry. He hit a few more keys and gave him another long, scrutinizing gaze. My heart skipped, and a bead of sweat wound down my cheek. The customs official slid Larry's passport back across the counter and nodded with a dispassionate expression. Larry was in, and I soon followed without any trouble. We both exhaled with relief and wove our way through the crowded terminal to our connecting flight to the city of Tabuk. Jabal al-Lawz was almost within our grasp.

TABUK

The yammer of male conversation rattled down the interior of the plane. It sounded to me as if everyone were embroiled in heated arguments, but it was customary, sociable Arabic communication. We had left Jiddah in an aircraft packed with travelers, and the hubbub of conversation made the cabin seem even smaller.

The men wore pressed white robes with headdresses and the traditional black *agal*. This standard article of Saudi attire reminded me of a car's fan belt. Centuries ago, Bedouin camel herders used similar headbands made of the rope to hobble the lead camel. When it was not around a camel's legs, the Bedouins used the *agal* to secure their scarves. The tradition had lasted for generations.

I tried to doze but found it impossible; I was still too amped. My heart hadn't settled down from the excitement of clearing customs a few hours earlier. Uneasiness clung to me like sweat. I still waited to feel a tap on my shoulder and hear, "You are under arrest. Come with me."

Larry sat next to me, a compass held flat in his palm. He had been staring at the small, wobbling needle for twenty minutes. I leaned over and watched the compass slowly rotate to the right. Larry frowned as the dial made a second revolution.

"We're flying in circles," he whispered. I looked out the window and saw nothing but the black velvet desert below.

A few minutes later, a distant cluster of lights came into view. It was our destination, Tabuk. The lights passed slowly by the plane's window, once for each revolution of the teetering compass needle. We were well over an hour late for landing, and that didn't bode well.

Larry tapped the face of the compass. "Something must be wrong."

We continued circling, the other passengers seemingly oblivious of the situation. I had been unsettled to begin with, and this wasn't helping.

There was an awful sound of twisting metal as the airplane jerked, then pitched as if seized by a giant hand. The engines roared as the pilots increased power. There was a surge forward, then the power dropped, and the plane began to plunge. Overhead bins popped open, disgorging bags of fruit, carry-on sacks, and luggage. A cascade of personal belongings fell into the aisle and onto stunned passengers.

Someone screamed.

The aircraft would free-fall, then recover a few moments later. It would heave to the left, then back to the right, snapping us around like a roller-coaster ride. One engine would roar, then another. I guessed that the pilot had lost some control of the flaps. If I was right, we were in a lot of trouble.

Panic spread, and I looked at Larry. He shrugged and gave an unconvincing smile.

"This does *not* look good." He would get no argument from me.

I looked out the window and was surprised and disturbed to see buildings. We were much closer to the ground than I had realized. Just below and coming fast were the runway and the beacon lights. An eternity of seconds later, the landing gear slammed onto the tarmac. The plane bounced and shuddered, its engines moaning painfully as the pilot reversed thrust. The front tires exploded on impact. A hideous screeching pierced the air as the big jet's bare wheel hubs gouged a groove in the runway. Sparks flew past my window.

The impact compressed my spine and drove the air from my lungs. I waited for the inevitable, whatever that might be. Finally, the plane shuddered and lurched to a stop at the end of the runway. My heart began to beat again.

Chaos filled the cabin. People were desperate to get off a plane that could burn at any moment; they crowded the aisles and pressed against the exit door. Larry and I waited for the stampede to subside. There was nothing else we could do.

There was more chaos outside. Fire trucks arrived, splashing the runway and the airplane with crimson light. Firemen in fire-protective proximity suits unfurled hoses and bathed the plane with white foam.

"Welcome to Tabuk," I said.

We deplaned safely. In the terminal we overheard talk of a hydraulic problem. We were fortunate in the outcome.

ON THE GROUND

At 3:00 AM, we climbed into a cab and gave our destination as the Tabuk Sahara Hotel. At that hour, I expected the small town to be asleep, its streets empty. Instead, couples strolled along the sidewalks, playgrounds were busy with children, and families were picnicking on the sandy highway median.

I had to ask, "What is everyone doing out at this time of night?"

The driver explained, "It's too hot in the daytime for the children to be out in the sun. They sleep all day and come out only at night."

I felt the knot in my stomach again. Larry and I planned to spend a week in a desert that was too hot for the locals.

After we checked into our hotel rooms, I collapsed into bed and did not wake up until midmorning on Friday, a weekend day for the Saudis. Our first order of business was to rent a truck and get enough provisions and supplies to sustain us in no-man's-land for at least a week. A cab took us into the business district of Tabuk, a drab, antiseptic town of gray-and-white cement buildings. We stopped at a truck-rental company. In front of the building, a camel knelt in the cargo bed of a small pickup—another reminder that I wasn't in Colorado. Larry spent twenty minutes signing papers, and soon we had a small white Datsun pickup truck.

When we went for supplies, the shop owners had closed their doors. Muslim culture requires compliance with prayer time. Although most followers are sincere in their faith, there is also a social pressure for shop owners to conform. Their patrons would view their absence unfavorably, and that might affect business. We would just have to wait. Once prayers were over, worshippers filled the streets and commerce resumed.

We foraged from shop to shop to supply our trek into the Saudi frontier. The back of our pickup was soon filled with canned meat, fruit, cases of bottled water, shovels, ropes, flashlights, batteries, and several twenty-gallon jerricans for gasoline reserves. We bought some Arab outfits of robes, scarves, and *agal*, foolishly thinking that we would then fit in among the desert Bedouins. Larry thought that instant-suntan lotion might allow us to blend in better. Unfortunately, the cream made our skin orange.

Our shopping complete, we retired to the hotel to cool off in the pool. There we quizzed each other on everything that could go wrong. We came up with countless scenarios and what-ifs. However many times we rehearsed our plan, I couldn't stop imagining two sets of bleached bones perched on a sand dune in the middle of nowhere, Larry clutching an empty canteen in his bony fingers and me holding a hand-scrawled note that said, "Obviously, we didn't think of everything."

The evening wind unleashed a sandstorm. It hurtled powerfully across the flat desert, sucking up grains of sand. There was nothing to blunt its advance. Outside the hotel, sand pinged off our window as the howling wind rattled the panes of glass. It was a great night to be indoors.

ON THE ROAD

Sleep was sporadic, but the winds finally subsided. Larry awoke with enthusiasm, eager to get to the mountain. We checked out of the hotel by 6:00 AM and headed into the predawn dark. The sun's orange disk soon spilled over the desert horizon, casting long shadows from dramatically furrowed rock formations.

We were crossing the ancient land of Midian, where the Bible says Moses met God at the burning bush on the slopes of Mount Sinai. Forty years before the burning bush experience, Moses had killed an Egyptian who was beating a Hebrew slave. When Pharaoh heard of this, he tried to kill Moses, but he escaped from Egypt and went to live in Midian, east of the Gulf of Aqaba in what is now Saudi Arabia.

We followed the snaking highway for two hours before finding our first landmark, the remote Al Kan gas station. Our wilderness turnoff was supposed to be four miles beyond that point, but there was no exit, no turnoff, and nothing that even resembled a road.

David Fasold's map showed a road at Al Kan, but all we saw in front of us was a wisp of trail stretching into the dunes and jagged mountains, barely discernible among the scattered rocks of the desert floor.

Within minutes, we were negotiating the floor of an immense desert valley that split into scores of narrow forks and wadis. Each subdivided the desert into dense clusters of winding ravines and stone-filled ditches. Every fifty yards or so we encountered huge rocks. Sand drifts and sagebrush blocked our path.

Maps were useless, and soon we knew that we were following the wrong path. We bounced and crunched through bruising ruts and scrub-filled ravines, bottoming out every few yards and fearing that at any moment we'd crack the oil pan and end the expedition.

The heat grew unbearable. Our small thermometer read 117 degrees, and it was only late morning. The thermometer would climb to 128 degrees in less than two hours, and our truck had no air-conditioning. Even if it did, the extreme temperature and the toiling exertion would overheat the engine.

The cab became a sweatbox. We rolled up our windows because

the heat blowing off the desert sand was unbearable. It was like looking down the barrel of a hair dryer. Larry and I sucked down prodigious amounts of water and occasionally poured the warm liquid over our heads. This soaking helped for only a few minutes. Dust seeped through the air vents, caking our sweaty skin with a gray, gritty film.

We weren't alone. We passed small Bedouin encampments, where pickup trucks hauling sheep, cases of supplies, and large tanks of water were engaged in the difficult work of desert commerce.

We lumbered deep into sheep country, frequently passing what looked like huge beach umbrellas raised several feet off the ground and tethered by ropes to tall poles. Tightly bunched herds of sheep huddled under these shelters, escaping the sun's ravaging rays in the tiny patches of shade.

We were lost. The desert that had been a few safe landmarks on a small map had become an immense foe that could easily consume us if we ventured farther into its sandy expanse.

Hoping to find our way back to the asphalt highway, I tried to turn the truck around. As I made the U-turn, the wheels of the truck left the two grooves of hard-packed sand and sank in the soft shoulder. Gunning the engine set the wheels spinning, spewing hot sand like a geyser. The truck sank to its axles. Without a word, Larry swung his door open to see how badly we were stuck. I joined him in surveying the situation.

We were trapped. The image of bleached bones seemed suddenly more vivid and real.

In desperation, I grabbed the rear bumper, planted my boots on the ground, and told Larry to gun the engine. I lifted and pushed, giving it all I had. Suddenly something snapped in my lower back.

Surging pain shot up my spine. For the next few seconds, I was unable to breathe. I clenched my teeth, stifled a scream, and dropped to my knees as if I had been shot.

Larry killed the engine and came around to the back. I assured him that I would be okay, but Larry isn't easily fooled. He saw the agony on my face. Larry started to say something when, seemingly out of nowhere, a pickup truck pulled near. Neither of us had seen or heard it coming.

It was a sun-faded, olive green jeep with a makeshift bed bolted on the back, crammed full of gawking kids. The driver, a robed man wearing a red-checkered *kaffiyeh,* stared at us for a moment in disbelief. His expression said, *What in the world are two white guys doing out here?* The robes and instant-tanning cream hadn't fooled him. He approached cautiously.

I imagine we made an unusual sight. Larry helped me to my feet as the Bedouin took in my pain and our immovable truck. He looked at me and then looked at the truck again. With a wave, he called the older boys from the truck, and they scampered over.

Bedouins have a desert code: they always help one another. If a stranger comes to a Bedouin's tent, the Bedouin is duty-bound by centuries of Arab custom to take the sojourner in as a guest. Larry smiled and bowed, gesturing to a big bag of oranges in the back of our truck. The man nodded, and soon every child had an orange. They were a big hit. The kids crawled out of the back of the jeep and began shedding the rinds, biting into the oranges like they were apples. They giggled as juice dripped from their chins and exchanged comments among themselves about the odd men who were stuck in the sand.

The Bedouin and the older boys walked to the truck and

rocked it from side to side. A small stream of sand trickled under the two left tires as the truck rocked right; when it rocked left, the right tires rose and sand filtered under them. After a few bouncing, sideways shoves, the truck rose up from the grasp of the desert. The father got in the truck, started it, and feathered the clutch while his sons pushed the vehicle free and onto the hard-packed road.

Larry thanked the man and boys profusely, bowing and shaking their hands.

"Can you take us to Jabal al-Lawz?" Larry asked. The smiles and celebration vanished.

The Bedouin's countenance darkened, and his gracious manner evaporated. A look of fear swept across his face as he talked quietly with the boys. One produced a pencil and paper and jotted down the license number of our truck. Clearly, something forbidden was associated with the mountain. I feared we might have crossed the line.

Larry was not so easily put off. After long and tense negotiations, he somehow persuaded the man to show us where the mountain was located in the chaotic jumble of peaks that surrounded us. In his jeep, our rescuer led us down a gentle slope and up a high, narrow ridge. Five minutes later, we were parked at the foot of a wide, sloping wall of granite, and our reluctant guide stepped from his truck. Crouching like an Indian scout in an old Western movie, he began crawling up the rock face. We followed, staying low as he maneuvered to a rocky crest overlooking a low, yawning plain. There, kneeling beneath the silhouette of a huge boulder, the Bedouin pointed toward something in the distance.

"Jabal al-Lawz," he whispered, as if unfriendly ears were nearby.

We peered over the valley. There it was—the mountain we had traveled so far to see. Rising majestically from the desert floor, it displayed two sharp, distinctively blackened summits.

We were finally looking at the real Mount Sinai.

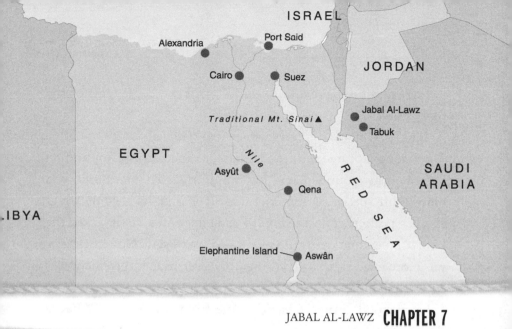

The Bedouin was agitated. He moved closer to me and pointed again toward the mountain. "Jabal al-Lawz."

"Jabal al-Lawz," I repeated, nodding.

Certain that we understood, he moved back down the rocky slope. The man who had come to our aid, who appeared confident and capable of handling our situation, now looked mortified and hollow. He negotiated the steep incline easily but seemed to be having trouble with the revelation he had given. I felt a measure of guilt. Had we presumed too much on the Bedouin culture so deeply rooted in the man? Had our cocky Western ways placed him on the horns of a social dilemma? Perhaps, but what was done was done. He had honored us twice, first by coming to our aid and now by disclosing the very thing we had risked so much to find.

Larry and I remained hunkered down behind the crest of the rocky knoll.

"That's . . . that's it," Larry whispered. "Jabal al-Lawz."

His tone captured my mood. I felt awe and surprise, joy and relief. My heart pounded, and my mind raced. The mountain was more than special; it was imperial. It wasn't its height; I had climbed peaks that dwarfed it. It wasn't its beauty, for it lacked the kind of splendor that would move a painter's soul. Nonetheless, it was more majestic than anything I had ever seen. Its grandeur was larger than life.

Larry stood abruptly, yanking me from my trance. "What is that?" He pointed.

I looked where he directed and saw a fence. In this land of open spaces stood a fifteen-foot-high fence topped with barbed wire. It appeared to stretch around the base of the mountain. It was a modern chain-link barricade set with galvanized poles. As a police officer, I had seen prison fences, and this wasn't much different. The last thing I expected to see in the middle of nowhere was a fence around a mountain.

"Why would anyone put a fence around a barren—"

The sound of a truck engine coming to life interrupted me. I turned to see our new friend pull away, leaving us in a cloud of dust. As I watched, he speedily rounded a bend without looking back. We had worn out our welcome.

"I guess Bedouins don't believe in long good-byes," Larry grumbled.

Our reluctant guide had abandoned us without a word. The abruptness of his departure concerned me. Had he gone off to inform the authorities? If so, we would soon know.

We returned to our Datsun, started the engine, and moved down the incline of the road as quietly as possible. We found a large, open basin. Not wanting to be too obvious, we parked in a small clearing behind a hill, out of sight of travelers who might use the valley trail.

It is difficult for a man to be calm and professional when he has stumbled upon the treasure he has been seeking, but Larry and I tried. We moved from the truck to the fence across open ground and found a large sign. The white letters on a blue background were written in English and Arabic and said, No Trespassing Allowed.

It was as if they had been expecting us. The bottom of the sign was notarized by the Saudi minister of antiquities, confirming that this was a restricted archaeological site. Seeing the fence and the sign made me think of David Fasold's letter. We knew that he had been to the site and that the Saudis had arrested him. There was a good possibility that this fence had been erected following Fasold's misadventure. The seizure of his notes and film had alerted the kingdom to the site's archaeological significance—and likely Jewish origins—and they had simply fenced it off to keep people like Larry and me out.

Months of planning, dreaming, hoping, and tens of thousands of dollars had led us to this mountain. Now a chain-link fence held us at bay. I studied the fence for a while. About a quarter mile to the north was a small concrete building. A guardhouse? Maybe. I wasn't going to go ask.

Had we really come halfway around the world only to be stopped by a fence? If this was really Mount Sinai, we expected a trove of hewn altars, pillars, ruins, and odd geologic anomalies, all of which needed documentation. We had to get inside the fence.

THE ALTAR OF THE CALF

We spent the next hour poking along the perimeter of the fence. Before we left the States, David Fasold had told Larry to look for a series of petroglyphs—ancient rock etchings of bulls or cows—on a pile of boulders. The boulders, he had said, appeared to be a construction, not a random accumulation of stones, and they were supposed to be in the valley we were exploring. Fasold thought that it was a religious site, perhaps the altar on which Aaron had placed the gold statue of the calf he had made.

Fasold's sketchy directions said, "From base of mountain, altar located east of second set of rutted tire tracks as they go up valley." This was no help at all. The rocks all looked the same, and too many tire tracks crisscrossed the terrain. Larry and I decided to split up in order to cover more ground.

My back had not let me forget what I had done to it. Spasms rolled through my lumbar region like storm-driven ocean waves, and at times I had to stop to catch my breath. I focused on the ground, concentrating on every step and hoping to loosen the wad of muscle constricting the base of my spine.

I hobbled over another rise and down a shallow swale. I had hiked to the shadowed side of the mountain and was thankful to be out of the sun. As I looked along the mountain's base and up its slope, my eyes fell on a huge pile of stacked granite. I blinked a few times to make sure I was seeing what I thought I was seeing. Large boulders sat one upon another as though a giant hand had placed them there.

It was an altar. More than that, I felt certain that I was looking at the most infamous altar in history. I could not imagine any set of natural circumstances that would account for their loose yet calculated arrangement. This man-made formation sat high on the otherwise pancake-flat plain, a totem to bygone events. A fence similar to that which surrounded Jabal al-Lawz encompassed it.

So close, and yet so far.

I wanted to speak, but no words came.

Another sign posted in Arabic and English warned trespassers to stay out. In my imagination, a new line formed at the bottom of the sign: This Means You, Bob. Considering our situation, I should have walked to a place where I could quietly get Larry's attention and wave him over. Instead, I cried out, "Larry! Larry! Over here!"

In the time that it took for Larry to appear, I inspected the size and configuration of the rocks. From every angle it remained an altar, clearly the result of human design, thick and imposing at the bottom and flat on top. The boulders were so large and unwieldy that hefting them into place would have required hundreds of able-bodied workers. I knew what could happen to a man just trying to free a truck stuck in the sand. These stones were placed by an orchestrated effort.

I took the Bible from my backpack and opened it, fanning the pages until I found the verse that was flashing neon bright in my brain—Exodus 1:11. The Old Testament book of Exodus tells how the Hebrew slaves were forced by their Egyptian masters to do bitter, backbreaking labor. The Hebrew slaves "built Pithom and Rameses as store cities for Pharaoh" (NIV). A people who could build cities could make a large stone altar like this one.

Larry came huffing over the rise. His khaki shirt and pants were shiny with sweat.

"Shhhh," he scolded as he approached. "Keep it down."

"Look." I pointed to the altar.

"I saw Bedouin guards and dogs behind the fence," Larry said in a sharp, low tone. "The guards had rifles. We've got to be careful. You can't just—just . . ."

His voice trailed off as his jaw dropped. I waited as he stood gawking, neck craned, taking in the sight. His face lit up.

We circled the stack of boulders, snapping photographs, noting its unique features, and stopping here and there to peer through the fence. The sharp contrast of the altar's dense shadows against the blinding sun made the petroglyphs hard to see, but they were there—ancient-looking engravings in the flat rock face. There was one of a bull, another of a calf. The most striking one was of a man holding a calf over his head, its spiraling horns replicating those of the ancient Egyptian Apis and Hathor bull gods. But why cattle? Why here? This wasn't cattle country. It was sheep country and had been so for as long as men had walked these plains.

Our search had just begun, but the presence of these engraved Egyptian cow deities on what must certainly be an altar was well beyond coincidence. It was important to be objective, but I couldn't help thinking that I was looking at the altar mentioned in Exodus. This was the place where the golden calf had offended God.

Larry went to get his metal detector. He wanted to see if any gold particles or residue had survived. The Bible states that Aaron melted the gold jewelry the Israelites had taken from Egypt to make the calf idol, and later, gold would be used in making the Ark of the Covenant. The gold had been given to the former slaves by Egyptians who, after ten horrible plagues, were glad to be rid of them. Because the Israelites had made the calf in haste, Larry thought that some gold might inadvertently have been lost. A hurried forging process might have been a sloppy one. The only way to know was to check.

Larry removed a suitcase-sized, state-of-the-art metal detector from the back of the truck. He had spent thousands of dollars on it, but he couldn't get it to work.

"It worked just fine when I tested it at home." His frustration was growing. Finally he removed the cover plate over the battery. His expression said it all.

"I forgot to bring the battery. A six-dollar battery!"

THE LONELINESS OF MIDIAN

We decided to camp for the night and then, if my back allowed, make our ascent up the back of the mountain away from the guardhouse. I tried walking, taking easy steps and hoping to limber up my back, but it cramped tighter. It was humiliating! My whole life I'd dealt with pain. I had played football in college and had learned how to put my dislocated shoulder back in joint to keep playing. As a policeman, I'd been banged around and beat up, but I just kept going. Now, standing where in all likelihood Moses once walked, I wondered if I would be able to get to my feet in the morning.

Our campsite was nestled into an S-shaped ravine, a perfect spot with plenty of shade and cover. No one could see us from the road, but we had a clear view of the back of the mountain, which helped to familiarize us with the terrain. Dinner was dried fruit and granola bars since a fire was out of the question. In the desert, any light is visible for miles. After a while, I limped off to a tilting rock to sit and collect my thoughts. I knew that the next day would hold the key to our success or failure.

The sun sank at its leisure. As it dipped toward the horizon, a slight breeze from the Red Sea slipped over the mountains. The stir of air cooled my sweat-soaked shirt, a welcome respite from the day of relentless heat. Without ice or air-conditioning, the water in our plastic bottles was always warm, like sipping water from a hot tub. The dying sun offered only a little hope that we could survive this inferno, and with my back still knotted in pain, I wondered if I would ever get to climb the mountain I had traveled so far to see.

The sun slipped behind the western hills, and the desert became still except for the whisper of wind. I glanced at my watch. It seemed that I'd been sitting motionless for hours, but the dial said that only ten minutes had passed. In the desert, time slows to a crawl.

I opened my Bible to the passage in Exodus that speaks of Moses' tending Jethro's flocks for forty years before God redirects him. Moses led, fed, and protected flocks of dumb, bleating sheep. He was eighty years old when God called him "to the far side of the desert" and gave him his marching orders. I couldn't imagine anyone lasting four decades in this vast wilderness. I was having trouble lasting a single day, and my fortieth birthday was a good way off.

In the distance, through fading twilight, I could see a shepherd tending a tiny flicker of a campfire. He was settling his flock for the night. That's when I realized that God had used this land to prepare Moses. He didn't use a prestigious university or a military academy. Instead, he used a demanding desert to forge the kind of character necessary for Moses to do the job—forty years of lonely, patient survival in the sand, sagebrush, and scorching sun.

The unsettling sense had been building in me that my being in this desert at this time, with pain searing my back, was forging something in me. I wasn't prepared for this moment, and I knew it. Unlike Moses, I wasn't equipped to stand on sacred soil. Encountering God was heady, soul-shaking work.

For some time, I had considered myself a believer in God. I wasn't a Bible thumper, but I had a growing understanding that the words in the Bible were true and verifiable if someone would just take the accounts at face value and go looking. Jim Irwin had started me down that path. The Bible had been his guide, and now it was becoming mine. I had heard Jim speak of his epiphany, of how he had stood in the gray soil of the moon and gazed across a quarter million miles of black space to see the blue-and-white globe that was the home of humanity. Wrapped in the protective cocoon of his space suit, he was as alone as a man could be, and yet he was not alone. Jim Irwin said that he encountered God on that desolate spot of the moon.

Now I was looking up from a desolate spot on earth to Jim Irwin's moon, which for a few moments had been his place of revelation. I knew that what Larry and I had found here in the desert would stay with me wherever my travels led me.

What would the coming hours bring? I had no idea. Would I be ready to climb that mountain as morning spread over the sun-bleached sand? Or was my journey over after all our intense preparation, effort, and intrigue? Had it boiled down to these few terrible hours of groping uncertainty, of hoping that I too might find my destiny on the far side of this sandy wilderness?

DAWN

Dawn breaks fast in the desert. Just before the sun's rays stretch across the desert floor, the heat slaps you with an open hand. There is no soft transition from the predawn chill, but an instant, prickly discomfort that rudely portends another day of relentless heat. On our first morning at the foot of Jabal al-Lawz, the sun began its journey from behind the jagged outline of the eastern mountains.

It was a moment of reckoning. I had spent the night in restless, uncomfortable sleep, my back refusing to forgive me for my previous bad decision. I have a phobia about snakes, so I had slept in the pickup, squeezing my bulky frame onto its narrow bench seat. I stretched my legs out one door and rested my feet on three boxes of water stacked beside the truck. My intermittent sleep became impossible when headlights from a rattling truck glared into our camp sometime after midnight. I heard some quick Arabic chatter, and then the truck backed off, leaving my senses even more ratcheted up. Every noise from the desert seemed threatening. Even the sound of Larry's high-tech, silver-foil Mylar space blanket crinkling and crackling at the slightest breeze was ominous.

I stood and tested my back with short, tentative steps. Despite the poor sleeping conditions, it had loosened somewhat, but it still throbbed painfully. I was far from healed, but at least I could stand, walk, and bend. I was going to climb Jabal al-Lawz. It wouldn't be easy, but the pain of staying would be worse than the pain of going.

After a quick breakfast of dehydrated fruit and bread, we filled our packs with water bottles, cameras, film, and protein bars. I found a six-foot cane pole left from a disbanded Bedouin camp and used it as a hiking staff.

We shuffled across a thin stretch of exposed valley to the base of the mountain. Unlike the east side of the peak, the mountain's backside was not fenced. We planned to climb up the back and come down the barricaded front, where most of our archaeological interest lay—along with the guards. We wore khaki clothing as camouflage against the sandy terrain and knew to keep a low profile. We figured that sooner or later the Bedouin patrols stationed nearby would spot us, but there was no reason to make it easy for them.

Thin trails fanned out before us like strands of a spiderweb. We chose a path up the hillside, then set a brisk pace on a surprisingly tame gradient. Jabal al-Lawz isn't a big mountain, and Larry and I had both done a fair amount of technical climbing. So in spite of an occasional sharp back spasm, it was an easy ascent for me. I pictured Moses, eighty years old when he ascended the peak for the first time, trudging stoically to the top without undue hardship. The most intimidating obstacles we faced were jagged rocks and stinging briars that made me glad we'd worn leather gloves. However, the gloves were no help against the cactus needles. Tiny spots of blood peppered my socks, pants, and shirt.

We backtracked once when we encountered impassable cliffs, then got quickly back on course, scrambling up an alluvial fan of loose gravel that ascended into a twisting ravine through fields of huge boulders and unstable scree. The trail dissolved near the top, so we clambered up the final pitch as best we could, forcing one foot in front of the other and sometimes going hand over hand, skirting rows of narrow ledges and stretching our bodies past sharp spires and fat outcroppings. There were some tricky moments. We shinned along a slick granite wall that angled over a sheer forty-foot drop. Our excitement overwhelmed caution and common sense.

Two hours into our climb, we reached the summit. Twin snub-nosed peaks were separated by a broad, rock-strewn bowl that pitched downward like a huge, open-air amphitheater. With each footstep, I wondered if I was crossing the stage on which the most extraordinary drama in human history had unfolded. As we strained over the last flinty hogback, we saw the stunning panorama of the desert below. As the tallest peak in the area, Jabal al-Lawz offers a spectacular vista of yellow-tinted hills and taupe plains fixed in ageless wind- and sand-sculpted shapes and textures. The morning sky was clear, and we could see for miles in all directions. To the west lay the faint, slate-tinted coast of the Red Sea; to the north and south, majestic mountain ranges bounded by broad desert.

Cresting a final step of crumbling sandstone terrace, Larry asked, "Do you think we're the first Westerners to reach this summit since the time of Moses?"

There was no way to know who had stood on the peak over the centuries, but it was a fair bet, and I was willing to believe it. We had crossed oceans and continents to stand on this peak, and it had seized our imaginations.

We had agreed to touch the top at the same time—a silly "all for one and one for all" mountain-climber thing. We were a team, and it was important for us to summit together. We counted in unison and planted our feet. It was a moment of celebration, of reveling in the probability that we were standing on one of the most historic places on Earth. We took several minutes to slap each other's back and congratulate ourselves, snap pictures, and just drink it in.

At 8,000 feet, we were standing near the place where Moses received the Ten Commandments. Was this not the unique place where God met with man in a lingering season of unprecedented intimacy and fearsome wrath?

Larry produced a piece of paper, and we both wrote a note to future travelers, extending our greetings and giving the time and date of our arrival. Then Larry placed the note in an empty plastic water bottle and buried it under some rocks. I thought it an excessive gesture, but for Larry it sealed the deal—it was a time capsule for posterity. I had my own business to tend to. I pulled from my pack a little tube containing a rolled-up American flag, one I'd taken with me around the world. I got the idea from Jim Irwin, who brought flags back from the moon. I had Larry snap a picture of me holding it on the summit, hoping to pass it on to my kids. I opened my Bible and wrote an inscription commemorating the day with a Scripture verse. "Then the Lord came down upon Mount Sinai, on the top of the mountain. And the Lord called Moses to the top of the mountain, and Moses went up" (Exodus 19:20).

THE SCORCHED BLACK PEAK

And then I remembered. In the bustle and excitement, I hadn't focused on the main feature that had gripped us from a distance—the strange dark crown that shrouded the summit with a shadowy stain. Glancing about, I immediately saw that the entire summit where we stood was unusually black. The rocks, and even the dirt, had a shiny tone like polished obsidian. The effect was startling, and we were genuinely baffled. We had hiked through acres of sagebrush and buff-and-beige sandy ridges to reach the top. That was all typical desert terrain, but now, at the summit, we stood on what appeared to be burned rock. What could have caused that?

The sun was rising. The Bedouins below were probably awake and steeping their breakfast tea. The early morning was quickly slipping away, so we collected as many loose rocks as our packs would hold for future laboratory analysis.

Larry seemed utterly mystified. "This has *got* to be a volcanic peak."

I could think of only one way to find out. "If it's volcanic," I said, "then the rock inside will be black, too. Right?"

"Makes sense."

I picked up a watermelon-sized piece of charred rock, lifted it over my head, and slammed it down hard on the sharp edge of a boulder. It cracked opened. My back protested, but I needed to know. We leaned in to look. The slick black exterior encased a reddish-tan core of ordinary brown granite.

Larry broke the silence. "Well, I guess that answers that question."

But it didn't add up. What type of heat could melt the surface of a rock to black marble, glazed and smooth to the touch like buffed opal, yet leave the underlying granite intact? Clearly, something intensely hot had torched the mountaintop. But what heat source could be potent enough to create a black rock rind while leaving a natural tan marrow?*

Larry was handling the rocks like fine china.

"There's something in the Bible about this." I took out my Bible and flipped through the pages. "Here it is," I said. "Exodus 19:16-19." I read aloud the account of how, three days after the Exodus party arrived at Mount Sinai, the mountain was mysteriously cloaked in a thick cloud, the skies above filled with thick clouds,

---

*Although most maps indicate that Jabal al-Lawz is volcanic, geological analysis of the rocks we brought back concluded that they were not volcanic but metamorphic. Metamorphic rocks are changed by recrystallization from extreme heat and/or pressure occurring after they are formed.

thunder, and lightning. "'Now Mount Sinai was completely in smoke, because the LORD descended upon it in fire. Its smoke ascended like the smoke of a furnace, and the whole mountain quaked greatly.'" There was more, but those few words said it all.

Seeing the rock and holding it, I could understand why the Israelites had been so frightened that they begged Moses to speak with God while they retreated to a safer distance. A holy, omnipotent God is an unbearable reality to an unruly people. And it was unbearable to me. I thought of the forgery I had been part of—the deceit and self-seeking stubbornness, the bullying aside of restraint and protocol to enter Saudi Arabia and strong-arm my way to this sacred soil. I was here illegally at a place so holy that God had told the Israelites not to touch the dirt at the base of the mountain or they would die (Exodus 19:12).

Shaken, I turned to Larry and urged, "Let's go. Now! We've got to get off this mountain." I grabbed my pack.

THE CLEFT OF THE ROCK

Larry placed the lens cap back on his Nikon. "I guess I've got all the pictures we need of the top," he said. I detected his hesitancy. He studied me as he had studied the rocks. "Are you all right?"

"Yeah. I'll . . . I'll be fine." I didn't know how to explain what I was feeling. "Let's just go."

Shuffling on hands and knees across the slippery scree, we paused briefly at the bowl-shaped amphitheater below the pinnacle as we searched for a path down the mountain. Tucked between the snub-nosed peaks was a hidden plateau, easily two football fields long. It was strewn with boulders larger than houses. Just below the second peak, a triangular monolith had formed from two large rocks tilted against one another. They formed a V, and in the crook or cleft of the V stood a lone almond tree, firm as a flagpole. I couldn't help but notice that this cleft was just wide and deep enough for a man to lie down inside. I recalled the words I had read in Exodus 33:21-22: "The Lord said, 'Here is a place by Me, and you shall stand on the rock. So it shall be, while My glory passes by, that I will put you in the cleft of the rock, and will cover you with My hand while I pass by.'"

THE RIVER

Halfway down the rocky face, we found a spacious table ledge concealed behind a tuft of cactus. It was the protected vantage point we needed to survey the front slope. We laid out our cameras, telephoto lenses, and binoculars and set to work, running down a checklist of man-made and natural features that should also be present if Jabal al-Lawz was the real Mount Sinai.

First, we had to find traces of a river. Deuteronomy 9:21 speaks of a brook or river somewhere on Mount Sinai, where Moses disposed of the crushed remains of the golden calf. He ground it to dust and threw it "into the brook that descended from the mountain."

Looking north across the grade, not twenty feet from our hidden perch, we saw a large ravine snaking down the mountain. It was an old riverbed. The meandering channel emanated from the mountain's west face, where it curled back and pitched steeply down the east-facing slope, emptying into the plain. In the ancient watershed, now the chalky remnant of a bygone wellspring, were large, water-smoothed boulders, clear evidence of water flow.

I checked that off the list.

THE CAVE OF ELIJAH

From our shelter, we turned to scan the upper peak. Had we missed something up there? The sun, now high in the sky, bathed the peak in its brilliant glare. Larry studied the upper heights with his binoculars while I reloaded the camera.

"There," he said. "Just below the second peak."

Squinting into the sun, I saw a cave sheltered beneath the lip of the plateau that overlooked the valley floor.

"How did we miss that?" I asked. The cave was obvious and no more than fifty yards from where we had stood looking at the cleft. First Kings 19:8-9 speaks of a cave on Mount Sinai used by Elijah to hide from Jezebel: "So he arose, and ate and drank; and he went in the strength of that food forty days and forty nights as far as Horeb, the mountain of God. And there he went into a cave, and spent the night in that place."

It was a crucial landmark. We could have kicked ourselves for not exploring it when we had the chance. Who knows what markings or petroglyphs it contained. Fear that we might already have been spotted prevented us from climbing back up. We would have to leave it for now.

STONE MARKERS

We turned our attention again toward the front slope and scrutinized it for the next hour. We might never have this opportunity again, and we didn't want to miss anything else like we had missed the cave. A scintillating array of features began to emerge. On the surrounding plain, an orderly series of sun-bleached rock piles encircled the front of the peak. We had bumped into a couple of these the day before but had thought they were Bedouin burial mounds.

From this elevation, we could see that they were stone markers, arranged at tidy, 400-yard intervals and forming a perfect semicircle about the mountain.

My pulse raced as I rifled through Exodus to chapter 19, verse 12: "You shall set bounds for the people all around, saying, 'Take heed to yourselves that you do not go up to the mountain or touch its base. Whoever touches the mountain shall surely be put to death.'" Those physical barriers were erected to spare humans and livestock the fatal fallout of God's fiery presence. Were these orderly stands of rock those sacred markers? An incredible collage was emerging as Mount Sinai revealed itself to us.

TWELVE PILLARS OF ISRAEL

"Check this out," Larry whispered in my ear. He pointed to the base of the mountain. "Look down there." He kept his binoculars pressed to his eyes. "You're not going to believe it."

I looked. Nestled against the bluff near the mouth of the ravine was an angular stone altar. It was a V-shaped structure, clearly man-made. The tip of one arm pressed into the fold of the ridge, and its companion slanted away at a forty-five degree angle. I estimated its length to be 120 feet. It was an altar of some sort, badly weathered and crumbling in spots, that stood five feet high and about twenty feet across. The remains of a central support wall ran the length of both arms of the V. Beside the altar in an almost straight line were what looked like the hewn stumps of stone pillars. Time and the elements had toppled them over, and they lay in broken sections, mostly near the altar.

I was now flipping pages again, racking my memory and searching for references. Exodus 24:4-5 gave a thrilling explanation of what we were looking at: "Moses wrote all the words of the Lord. And he rose early in the morning, and built an altar at the foot of the mountain, and twelve pillars according to the twelve tribes of Israel. Then he sent young men of the children of Israel, who offered burnt offerings and sacrificed peace offerings of oxen to the Lord."

This must be the altar, sitting precisely at the foot of the mountain, that Moses had built in preparation for Israelite worship. I counted the pillar stumps—there were twelve of them.

"That is the altar and pillars where the Israelites offered burnt sacrifices to God."

Larry started snapping away with his telephoto lens. "Incredible," he said between clicks of the shutter. "This is amazing."

I agreed. We had taken the Bible at face value, with no agenda to prove. All we wanted was to find the real Mount Sinai. I did a quick mental inventory to make sure the pieces were fitting: scorched and blackened peak, an ancient riverbed, a cave, a massive stone altar, twelve pillars, sacred markers, and a curious cleft in the rock. It was all there. We could add to our evidence the statement in Galatians 4:25 that said Mount Sinai is in Arabia. Jabal al-Lawz is next to a desert, with nine direct points of connection between the ground upon which we stood and the place described in the Bible. I couldn't forget the large stone altar with the petroglyphs that I had seen the day before. The number of confirmations continued to rise.

No single item—the cave, the dry wash—could have demonstrated that this was Mount Sinai, but finding so many correlating pieces of evidence was beyond coincidence. Cecil B. DeMille could have filmed *The Ten Commandments* here without moving a stone.

I had spent several years of my adult life as an investigative detective. I understood the burden of proof "beyond a reasonable doubt" that was needed to secure a criminal conviction. I had been trained to connect tiny, seemingly unrelated bits of evidence into a winning verdict. One drop of blood or piece of thread can turn the decision in a criminal case. In my opinion, the case for Jabal al-Lawz would win in any courtroom. If we had spotted just one or two unique anomalies, I might have had doubts. The scorched mountaintop, the man-made altars, the petroglyphs, the pillars, and the stone markers were stunning in and of themselves, but it was the sum of these things that testified to the site's authenticity.

As I sat up and stared across the plain, an arresting scene began to unfold. I imagined the flickering glow of thousands of Israelite campfires warming the valley. I pictured Hebrew children playing beside their tents and livestock kneeling to drink beside a huge reservoir carved into the plain. The official name of the mountain is Jabal al-Lawz, but I was now convinced that it was Mount Sinai, the site of one of the most amazing stories ever told.

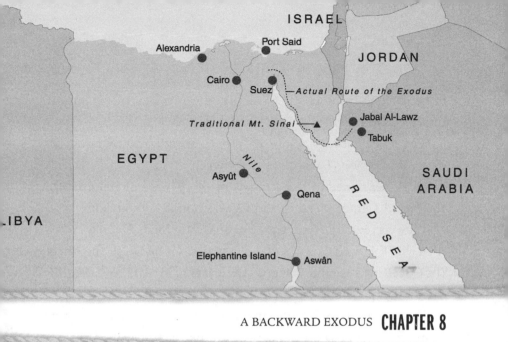

It was well past noon when we again scanned the valley floor with our binoculars, making certain that we had not overlooked any anomalies. We started down the mountain, descending on foot when we could and sliding on our seats when we couldn't. We skidded to a stop at the bottom, with gaping holes in our bloodstained pants. We sprinted past the last jagged ramparts and gullies to the peak's unguarded backside.

It was still a mile-long hike to our campsite. We walked briskly through a washboard basin, dry washes, and stubble-filled wadis, keeping our heads low and watching for Bedouin patrols. Along the way we saw small almond trees. The Bible tells of the almond rod that budded for Aaron at Mount Sinai. Certainly too much time had passed for any of the ones we saw to be the tree from which Aaron's rod was taken, but it got my imagination flowing.

We passed through scattered groves of odd, thorny trees. On closer inspection, I realized that they were acacia trees. Acacia wood is mentioned in Exodus as a primary building material for the sacred Tent of Meeting and its ceremonial contents. It was an obscure yet revealing find. Camped at Mount Sinai, Hebrew craftsmen who followed God's detailed instructions had built the Ark of the Covenant, the table it sat on, the altars of incense, and even the sacred tent poles and crossbars from acacia wood.

Three-quarters of a mile into the plain, we thought we were home free. Less than a quarter of a mile separated us from our truck and a hasty retreat from this forbidden valley. For the first time in days, I allowed myself to relax, but this was premature. From our left came sudden voices, followed by a loud gunshot that echoed down the wadi like a cannon report.

"Oh man, what now?" Larry said.

We walked a few more feet, then stopped and waited. There was a loud shout in Arabic. We stepped up from the gully into a small clearing and came face-to-face with two men in military garb. The taller, older man held a 12-gauge shotgun in his arms. At the sight of it, I forgot my back pain.

"Let's just try to stay cool," I whispered. The words had to pass a huge lump in my throat. This was the living, breathing embodiment of my worst fears—armed Saudis in uniform.

"*Marhaba*," I said with a smile. This meant "hello" in Arabic.

I waited for a response. In those moments, I wasn't sure if they were soldiers on patrol or simply bandits who would steal our expensive equipment and cut our throats. Neither was a good option.

Their baffled glances told me that they didn't know what to make of two filthy, sweaty, sunburnt Americans strolling in the desert. We offered them some of the food and water we were carrying. The tall one—an unshaven, ragged-looking character with terrible teeth—made short work of our last water bottles.

Larry cut to the chase. He gestured toward their gun and mimicked a man shooting birds from the sky. "Bang! Bang! Bang!"

They laughed and nodded as if to say, "Yes, we are hunters."

My heart slowed a beat. Maybe they weren't soldiers or bandits but simply two young Bedouins shaking the brush for quail. Carefully gauging their response, we smiled and waved, as if to say good-bye, then started walking toward the campsite.

Our fears subsided when they strolled off in the opposite direction and disappeared behind some rocks. Larry and I made a dash for the truck, hoping for no more impromptu meetings with armed Bedouins.

Our relief was short lived. As we crested the final knoll overlooking our campsite, we saw another pickup parked beside ours. We climbed down to the edge of our camp to find the same Bedouins rifling through our boxes and suitcases and throwing papers and notebooks from the glove box. I concluded that they were soldiers after all, sent to search our stuff and arrest us for trespassing. Either that or they meant to rob us, shoot us, and leave our corpses to rot.

Luckily, we had wrapped and buried anything that might be incriminating—tools, maps, travel notes on Jabal al-Lawz—under a rock by the truck. They were more aggressive now, and we guessed that they wanted to know who we were, where we were from, and what we were doing there. We flashed our passports and showed them our letter from the Saudi prince. We began calmly retrieving our belongings and put them in the truck, holding our breath to see their reaction.

The suspense ended as quickly as it began. Perhaps the Saudi royal signature on that letter had spooked them. For whatever reason, they hopped into their truck and drove away. They offered no good-byes, but I didn't care. I was just glad they were gone.

"Let's get out of here," Larry said, throwing his pack into the back of the pickup. He didn't need to ask twice. In less than five minutes, we were packed and bouncing along the rutted dirt path away from the mountain. We studied our maps, then set a course for the Red Sea, where we hoped to find the mysterious underwater land bridge that stretches across the gulf from the tip of the Sinai Peninsula to the shore of Arabia. We had seen it from the Sinai Peninsula; now we wanted to see it from this side of the Gulf of Aqaba. We were traveling the Exodus route backward.

As we left the mountain, I knew we were in all likelihood passing the place where the Ark of the Covenant had been constructed. Inside the Ark had rested the stone tablets of the Ten Commandments that Moses had received on Mount Sinai. My heart beat a little faster as I realized that I might have been standing on holy ground.

THE SPRINGS OF ELIM

As far back as when we had sketched our first rough itinerary in Los Angeles, the town of Al-Bad had figured into our plans. It lay strategically between Jabal al-Lawz and the Straits of Tiran, in the dead center of a broad valley. If our theory was correct and the Israelites traveled this valley on the path to Mount Sinai, they would have passed through Al-Bad. We decided to look around.

The thirty-kilometer drive to Al-Bad took two hours. The map showed no direct roads, so we backtracked to the Al Kan gas station and took the asphalt road that looped the densely packed mountains. Approaching the town, we saw a grove of palm trees like fingers reaching for the sky. We also saw sparkling water in concrete reservoirs near ground level. They seemed to sprout magically in the middle of the withering desert. We had run across a true oasis in the sea of baked earth.

"Does this ring a bell?" I asked Larry.

He shrugged and shook his head. "Should it?"

"The Bible describes two significant stop-off points along the path from the Red Sea to Mount Sinai." I explained that the first was a spring where the water was too bitter to drink. The second was a rejuvenating oasis between the Wilderness of Shur and the Wilderness of Sin.

I parked the truck and strolled beneath the dense canopy of palms, relishing the shade that held the heat at bay. I knelt at one of the primitive cisterns and raised water to my mouth with a cupped hand. I had never tasted better water. Drinking turned to splashing as we poured water over our heads, across our necks, and down our backs until our clothing was drenched.

Refreshed, I returned to the truck. I searched my Bible for Exodus 15:27 and read it to Larry. "'Then they came to Elim, where there were twelve wells of water and seventy palm trees; and they camped there by the waters.'" I looked around. "This may be the same place."

Elim was near the home of Jethro, Moses' father-in-law, who lived in the region of Mount Sinai. I could count approximately seventy palms. Then I walked around the wells and counted exactly twelve springs.

The sun was beating down with a vengeance, making us reluctant to leave the shade and cool water. *What an amazing land,* I mused, *where thirty-five-hundred-year-old treasures keep emerging from the sands.* These cryptic trail markers had been fixed in time, waiting through the centuries for someone to connect the dots. There was an oasis along the true Exodus route. If the mountain we had left behind was the true Mount Sinai, and if we were traveling the ancient path of the Exodus in reverse, then finding an oasis made sense. Could such an oasis survive for over three millennia? There was no reason to believe that it could not.

We left with the amazing thought that we might have just refreshed ourselves at a resting place of Moses and his followers.

"MOSES WAS HERE!"

The town of Al-Bad wasn't much more than a small village of dusty shanties and uneven tent rows, with a population of perhaps five hundred people. But this inconsequential dot on a map seemed invaluable to me. This oasis in northwest Saudi Arabia is the ancient city of Madyan (Midian), known throughout the Muslim world as the hometown of Jethro, Moses' father-in-law.

In town, we parked on the main street, hoping to find someone who could tell us about the ruins indicated on our maps. Larry and I entered one shop after another, only to see owners fast asleep on the floor, either snoozing from sun-induced lethargy or because any possible patrons were at afternoon prayers, or both.

We finally found someone awake in a modest, ill-stocked grocery store at the end of the road. A neatly dressed young Arab approached and offered his assistance.

"I couldn't help overhearing your English," he said. "Can I be of help?"

His English was impeccable, and he responded to our compliments by explaining that he had been reared and educated in Syria. I mentioned that we were trying to find the ruins noted on our map.

"Oh yes. The ruins you speak of are located about five kilometers north of town. They are the caves of Moses."

"The caves of who?" Since Moses is so closely tied to Judaism, I was surprised to hear a Muslim mention the name with pride. "You said the caves of Moses? How do you know this?"

"Everyone around here knows that the Prophet Musa camped at the town of Al-Bad. It's part of this town's heritage."

"Let me get this straight," Larry said skeptically. "Caves of Moses? Here?"

"Yes, it is well-known," the Syrian replied, explaining that he was a translator for a Saudi archaeologist who—of all the wild coincidences—happened to be excavating those very caves. It was an eerie, incredible stroke of good fortune to have bumped into this walking tourist brochure for the ruins we wanted to see.

Larry asked me if the Bible made any mention of caves where Moses lived.

"Not that I know of," I said.

"The Prophet Musa has always been a part of this region's history. Moses' father-in-law, Jethro, pitched his tents near this oasis. In fact, markings and writings in those caves tell us that Jethro and Moses' wife, Zipporah, were buried in tombs in the hillside. The people are very proud of their heritage."

Tombs? Markings? Moses, a local hero? I was confused. Why would Moses, a Jewish prophet, be celebrated in a Muslim country? I asked this and got a quick response.

"Moses was a Muslim prophet as well," he explained. "It is in all of our literature. Moses camped at the oasis of Al-Bad before moving on to Jabal al-Lawz, the Mountain of Moses."

"You . . . you mean Mount Sinai?" I said.

The Syrian nodded. "Yes, Mount Sinai. It sits a short distance north of here."

"How do we get to the caves?" Larry asked.

The Syrian raised a hand. "I urge you gentlemen not to approach the caves. There are soldiers camped there. It is fenced off and heavily guarded. It is forbidden."

"How exactly would one find these caves, assuming someone were foolish enough to want to visit?" I asked.

At first our Syrian friend wouldn't budge, unwilling to be party to our arrest. He finally relented and directed us toward the ruins.

He looked very nervous.

THE CAVES OF MOSES

We parked the truck behind a dune and got out. I was hoping to snap a few photos of the caves. As we stood admiring the fascinating array of caves and ruins, a car pulled up and parked forty feet behind us. The driver, a short, stocky man, marched over and introduced himself. He was a Scottish engineer wearing, of all things, a heavy plaid flannel shirt. He said he was doing some work for a Philippines-based engineering firm and seemed eager to chat. He looked at our cameras.

"You'd better not be seen with those, lads." He grinned, reached into his vest pocket and removed a tiny automatic camera and snapped a quick series of photos.

"Just who are you?" I asked. There was something about him.

"I'm also a pastor doing some research. Those caves over there are the caves of Moses."

"Yes, we know," I said.

I started to ask another question, but before I could, the Scot had dropped the small camera back into his pocket, bid us a cheery farewell, and driven off, saying, "Take caution, lads." His car vanished in a spray of dust.

We stood there wrestling with the pros and cons, brainstorming every possible scenario for reaching the caves. There were soldiers milling about, and the place was overrun with bulldozers and men in hard hats at work in front of the caves. We had no idea what they were doing but agreed that so many soldiers were reason enough to exercise restraint. After a last long look back, we drove toward the coast to find the spot directly across from Sharm al-Sheikh. This, we surmised, would be where the Israelites had climbed onto Arabian soil after walking through the Red Sea.

BITTER SPRINGS

The only route to the coast is a reasonably well-maintained one-lane asphalt roadway that cuts through the flats of a broad valley. This natural byway would have offered the Israelites an accommodating passage on their northward trek toward the mountain. The look and feel of the topography gave us good reason to expect at least one more tantalizing find on our drive south. I had already alerted Larry that the Hebrews had made two historic rest stops on their trek to Mount Sinai, the first being the bitter springs of Marah.

The record reads, "So Moses brought Israel from the Red Sea; then they went out into the Wilderness of Shur. And they went three days in the wilderness and found no water. Now when they came to Marah, they could not drink the waters of Marah, for they were bitter. . . . And the people murmured against Moses, saying, 'What shall we drink?' So he cried out to the Lord, and the Lord showed him a tree; and when he cast it into the waters, the waters were made sweet" (Exodus 15:22-25). Could we find something that fit those words?

Leaving Al-Bad, we reset the odometer to zero. Scripture says that after crossing the Red Sea, the Israelites traveled for three days without finding water, and that when they came to Marah, they could not drink its water because it was bitter. We figured that at twenty kilometers south of Al-Bad we would be approximately three days' walk from the coast. At twenty kilometers, nothing appeared. We drove another five kilometers, then ten, driving slowly to survey the land. Nothing. Then, just as we were about to turn around, we saw a dry, mud-caked flat in the distance. It appeared to be the remnant of a large, long-gone lake. On closer inspection, we saw that it actually consisted of several dry basins spanning dozens of square miles. Their sizes varied from large lake beds to very small ponds. All of them were concentrated in a chalky, low-lying depression that would collect water during wet seasons.

Scattered across the plain and poking up like giant anthills were smooth-faced, alkali-encrusted mounds, some standing as high as three feet. Hiking the area, we saw that they were primitive wells formed of packed mud. They were left from the days when the locals still dug into the shallow aquifer. Some of these wells were shallow, while others were as deep as eight feet. Their interior walls were scarred and grooved from ropes used to raise and lower buckets.

I dipped a finger into a shallow well and touched it to my

tongue. It was vile and caustic. A single drop was so acidic that it made my teeth ache. Unless these Bedouins had cast-iron stomachs, they couldn't drink this stuff.

I looked at the rope marks. "Why would anyone want to draw this water?"

"They probably water their sheep with it," Larry suggested. He knew from his Montana youth that sheep thrive on hard alkaline water known to poison other livestock. He tasted the water, and his scowl said more than words. The water's extreme bitterness fit the narrative better than we had expected.

The size of the basin was large enough to accommodate the Hebrew multitude, and its thirty-five-kilometer distance from the Straits of Tiran coincided closely with the Israelites' three-day walk from the Red Sea.

I wondered what the scene must have looked like. Upward of two million people and uncountable livestock traveled across this plain. Their water was running low, the sun was high and hot, and they were uncertain of their future. It was more than my mind could take in.

Were these the Springs of Marah? The evidence suggested that it could be. As with everything else, there was no way for us to prove it, but coincidence didn't seem like an unreasonable explanation.

Stress, heat, and an almost total lack of sleep were taking a toll on me. We drove on, hoping to reach the Straits of Tiran before dark.

THE FLIP SIDE OF AQABA

It seemed more dreamlike than real, standing on the east shore of the Gulf of Aqaba and gazing across its waters to the edge of the Sinai Peninsula. Not long ago, I had stood on the far shore with

Larry and Jim Irwin. We had dived the reef that bound these two points together and had discussed the letter that would set our present search in motion. It seemed a century ago.

From the Arabian side, I could see across the gulf to the tip of the Sinai Peninsula. The jutting mountains rimmed the wide beach, and the twinkling lights of Sharm al-Sheikh blinked through the ashen dusk.

The panorama of the Exodus materialized before me. The crowd gathered on that distant beach would have stretched for miles, with their leader, Moses, standing at the water's edge. The Egyptian army was advancing from the southwest, coming around the tip of Sinai. The people, seeing no hope for survival, were terrified. The mountains blocked them to the north and west, and the only place to go was into the sea.

Moses raised his staff, and the Red Sea split into what the Bible describes as two walls of water. The children of Israel passed on dry ground between the surging bulwarks of the sea. The Egyptians followed them into the sea, and God collapsed the water onto them.

Flavius Josephus, the first century-Jewish historian, described the Exodus in his *Antiquities of the Jews:* "There was on each side a ridge of mountains that terminated at the sea, which were impassable by reason of their roughness, and obstructed their flight; therefore they there pressed upon the Hebrews with their army, where the ridges of the mountains were closed with the sea."[2]

Josephus's words match the area around Sharm al-Sheikh perfectly.

Our journey was about over, and I was glad. I was filthy, tired, and sore. We hadn't bathed since the Tabuk Sahara, and we reeked. Before us was a delightful blue sea with a deserted shore. We quickly stripped to our underwear and raced down the sandy beach. The water was cool and indescribably welcome. Nothing had ever felt so good.

Toweling off on shore, we realized how badly sunburnt we were. Tiny red welts tattooed my wrist where the sun had burned through the weave of my watchband. Larry's face was the hue of sun-dried tomatoes. These paled alongside our blush of personal triumph. We built a fire from dead scrub, dined on dehydrated beef stroganoff, and settled down for the night.

The day before, we had climbed the tallest mountain in Midian, where God and man had talked face-to-face. Today we were probably at the very spot where the Israelites had emerged from the Red Sea. For those few moments, I tried to convince myself that God was well pleased with our efforts—or at least with our stubborn persistence.

THOUGHTS OF HOME

The fire soon consumed the parched brush we had gathered, and the embers expired. Larry and I were lost in our private thoughts, staring silently out into the Gulf. In the clear night, I could easily see the Egyptian shoreline. Seeing it from such a distance somehow reminded me of how homesick I was. It seemed that we had been on this adventure for months, and it felt at least that long since I had hugged my wife and children.

On the hill above us, lights from a small mosque winked down on the waters. Farther up the shoreline and nestled into a sandy ridge was the dark shadow of a military pillbox—a bunker no doubt left from the Six-Day War.

I'd had my fill of Saudi Arabia. I was tired of the secrecy, frustrated by the language barrier, and stressed by the ever-present threat of exposure and arrest. I was sick of the heat, the dust, and the desert. I had only been here for a week, but if I never had to return to this sweltering, dusty desert, it would be too soon.

At that moment my thoughts turned toward the wandering Hebrews. A terrible sadness blanketed me. They had stood here on a day of worship and rejoicing. God had delivered them from Pharaoh's grasp and from certain, cruel death. They had witnessed the miracle of the ages, having walked through the Red Sea to new freedom and a new beginning.

It was their sweet moment. What followed was forty years of bitterness, brutal hardship, and war. Lying on the beach, staring out at the waves, I knew what awaited them—and it wasn't pretty. We had just been through the bitter springs, the endless desert, and the indescribable heat. They would face strife and dissension. Families would be torn apart, and the nation would be under continual attack from fierce tribes. They would taste the numbing futility of walking circles in a scorching desert and see their most stalwart warriors struck down, the hearts of their bravest men turned to wax. The dream of a Promised Land lay before them, but most of them would never see it. Their bodies would be buried in the dust before their children could embark on their promised new life. What cruel drudgery it must have been for them to languish those forty years in these bitter badlands.

Unlike those Hebrews, Larry and I could go home satisfied. We had accomplished what we had set out to do. I could smell the crisp Colorado mountain air, and I was ready to leave. My admiration for those people of the past was forever cemented in my mind. The Exodus was no longer just a Sunday school story for me.

UNFINISHED BUSINESS

The Datsun was falling apart. It seemed that every strut, screw, and rivet holding it together was shaking loose. We were clattering down the highway toward Tabuk. All four shock absorbers were grinding and squeaking on their pins. Then one snapped off and began dragging on the ground with a clattering screech that set my teeth on edge. All four tires and rims had endured so much pounding that they wobbled on their axles.

Larry and I weren't in much better shape. Every time we hit a rut or a bump, I winced. My back had still not forgiven me. Sunburn had turned my skin to broiled salmon. Larry was stoically nursing his own collection of cuts, scrapes, and contusions. All I could think of was getting back to the Tabuk Sahara, ordering a nice room-service dinner, falling asleep with the air conditioner going full blast, and booking our flight home.

Crumpled against the passenger door, Larry was a pitiful sight. I took it for granted that he was as eager to get home as I was. We were traveling back on the same road we had taken in. I could see the old Al Kan gas station a mile or so ahead where the turnoff to Jabal al-Lawz was located.

"Hey, Bob," Larry said. "I've been thinking. We should go back to the mountain and see what's inside that fence."

"What?" I jerked my head around and looked at him. He had lost his mind! "You're kidding, right? Our truck is broken-down. I'm broken-down. So you're kidding, right? Tell me you're kidding."

He wasn't.

"I was just thinking that we're being premature," Larry said, as if he were discussing a business decision. "I mean, are we fooling ourselves? Did we really get all the evidence we need to prove our case? Would our findings hold up in a court of law?"

I said nothing. The truth was that I couldn't think of anything to say.

He continued casting doubt on the quality of the pictures we had taken. "All I'm saying is, I think we need more. We took some of those shots from quite a distance."

Larry made his best case, but I wasn't buying it. I didn't want to think about taking the turnoff ahead of us. I didn't want to go back into that hellish desert even if we hadn't taken convincing photos. I, too, had thought that we needed to get inside the fence and have a closer look at the pillars and altars. I had hoped to see inside the cave of Elijah and to get better, closer shots, but the truth was that I was spent. At the turnoff, I just kept driving, passing it by. I drove on in silence, jaw clenched and eyes glued to the road.

"Larry," I said as diplomatically as I could, "we've got more than enough evidence." Then we stared out of the cracked windshield as a tense hush filled the cab.

I prevailed because I was driving. Larry leaned against the passenger door and said nothing more until we had checked into our hotel. I wasn't concerned. I figured that the heat had temporarily fried his brain. Now that we were back in the comfort of our room, I was sure that he was relieved that I had cast the dissenting vote. It was an uncomfortable way to end our adventure, but I was just glad that we were going home.

We got out of the kingdom with relatively little resistance. There were long, nerve-racking customs lines as we waited to see if the authorities would allow us to leave or if they would haul us off to prison. None of my nightmares had come true. At the

Tabuk Sahara, we had wrapped our film and rock samples in enough layers of filthy socks and dirty underwear to discourage any customs agent. The worst moment was at the international terminal in Jiddah. A customs agent, poking through my bags with a long stick, found my dog-eared leather Bible. He began thumbing through it, then turned to the New Testament. He noted the first pages of the book of Matthew, then closed the book. He looked into my eyes. "I can see you're not Jewish," he said. "You can go."

Larry's scare came in the same customs line. He forgot the name of our fake Saudi sponsor and had to wing it on the exit questionnaire. But these proved to be minor interruptions. We passed through like clockwork to the comforting sound of the official stamping our visas.

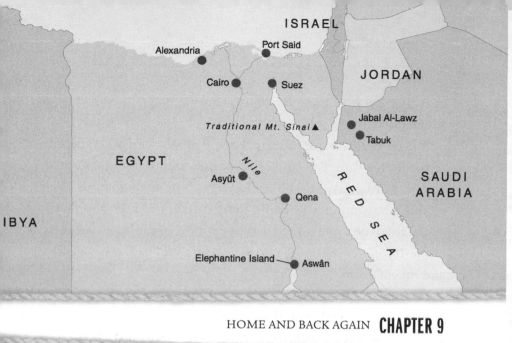

Colorado, 1988

I was home and I was miserable. I had added one more adventure to my life and had gone where few had gone before. My perspective had been changed, and it continued to change as I rethought each step of the adventure and everything that we had seen. Jim Irwin and the others who had said that Mount Sinai must be in Saudi Arabia were right.

I had walked beneath a blazing sun, dodged guards, endured setbacks, and achieved what I set out to do. Yet I was still unhappy. I sat in the comfort of my home. I appreciated my own bed, soaked up the love of my family, and walked familiar ground. I had every reason to be content, with more blessings than I could expect or deserve. Still, there was a niggling awareness that not only had I let an opportunity pass, but I had let a friend down in the process.

When I signed on for this trip, Larry had asked for and expected to receive my full effort, and I had promised it to him. He wanted and needed a gutsy guy who could forge ahead in tough times. Yet in those last minutes when he needed the kind of a guy that I promised to be, I had turned for the comfort of the hotel and then home. It took a while for me to realize this, but I had let both Larry and myself down.

It is difficult for some to understand, but I had betrayed an unwritten professional code that was deeply engraved in my mind and heart. As a cop, I had frequently called for backup to help with a dicey situation, and I never doubted that it would come. When I was called upon to back up others, I made sure that I was there for them. That is what cops do. I could count on others and they could count on me.

Back in that distant land that seemed more a dream than reality, when our Datsun groaned with every bump and threatened to fall apart beneath us, I was called upon to go the extra mile, to go back to the mountain to make certain we had done it right.

And I had said no.

Those words haunted the dark corridors of my thoughts.

To make matters worse, Larry called and told me that his photos were unconvincing. There was too much to see, too much to take in. We would have had better luck trying to capture the grandeur and magnitude of the Grand Canyon in a single shot. Our amateur photos were disappointing, just another reminder that Larry had been right and I had been wrong. Many of the features we had photographed were a mile or more down the slope of Jabal al-Lawz.

The terrain was so vast that it was impossible to gauge the scale of objects, such as large altars and pillars. Set against the expanse with nothing familiar to provide scale, these magnificent objects looked insignificant.

A bile-like sense that it had all been for nothing rose in me.

"Listen, Bob, I can barely convince my friends and family with these shots, and if we can't convince them, then—"

He didn't need to finish the sentence. Larry was gracious and didn't chastise me for refusing to go one more round, but sometimes kindness hurts more than blunt speech. Then he issued the challenge. "What's behind that fence, Bob? I want to know what they're hiding." There was a pause, then, "Let's go see what's back there. If we believe—I mean really believe—that Jabal al-Lawz is Mount Sinai, then we must get behind that fence. If we don't do it now, it will eat at us the rest of our lives. If this is the real Mount Sinai, then we are making history."

It was an impassioned, unnecessary plea. His thoughts were my thoughts. I had developed a desire to go back that had grown into a need. How could I say no? It was the only way to get the job done.

For years I had complained that many scholars sit in dusty libraries making pronouncements about what is and isn't true, unwilling to risk the unknown to make their own verification. If I didn't want to eat my own words, I would have to step out again. I wanted to go because I wanted to know. I needed to redeem a promise to my friend. I was compelled by the enormous implications of a discovery that awaited completion.

There was a tug on my mind and heart. Intellectual and emotional reasons both had a part in my decision. I had a vague sense that something spiritual was also in the mix. It is impossible to quantify such things, but the bottom line was that we were going back.

This time we would know what lay ahead of us. This trip would be easier to plan, and we should be able to get in and out in less time with the photos needed. Larry insisted on footing the bill and already had the visa process under way. Somehow he knew I would say yes.

"Okay, Larry, I'll go back, but this time let's get proper entry visas. If we're going to do it, then let's do it right."

THE RETURN

The full moon washed Jabal al-Lawz in ivory light, lending the contours of rocks and shrubs a pearly translucence. In the distance, sheepdogs barked and howled at unseen things in the darkness.

"Sounds like they caught a scent," I said.

"I hope it's not us," Larry answered.

He had a right to be concerned. We had come face to ugly face with the ferocious breed earlier that day. We had been on the road from Tabuk to the site when we stopped to get our bearings. While we scanned the area for landmarks, a snarling, slobbering dog charged us from behind a rock outcropping. We scrambled into the car before Cujo could get his first taste of American flesh. The dog's face smashed into my rolled-up window, snapping and foaming at the mouth.

"I think it wants to eat me right through the glass," I shouted, my heart pounding like a piston.

"Let's get moving before he bites through the tires."

We were back in the Saudi kingdom, on the road we had traveled less than two weeks before. Once I had embraced the idea of returning, I had poured myself into a whirlwind schedule of preparation and planning. This time, however, our visas posed no problem. The Saudi prince had returned and promptly provided a letter of sponsorship. Using his London contacts, Larry fast-tracked our paperwork through the Saudi embassy. It seemed that we had barely returned to the States when we were back on a plane to Jiddah, then Tabuk. We touched down in Tabuk shortly after sunrise. This time we didn't bother with a hotel but rented a truck, bought our supplies, and drove straight to the mountain.

This time there were no miscues; there was no getting stuck. We knew the way, knew what we needed, and knew what to expect. We cruised past the sand pit where I had injured my back and arrived at the mountain by late afternoon. Rather than approach the mountain's exposed backside as before, we drove straight to its east face—the portion protected by the chain-link fence. We stayed low and out of sight by driving slowly into a low-lying depression until we reached a crescent-shaped stand of rocks. About a quarter mile across the valley from the altar of the golden calf, we hunkered down in the wadi just out of sight of the guardhouse, waiting for dark.

To minimize the risk of guards spotting us, we planned a nighttime excursion. We had invested in a pair of infrared night-vision binoculars in London.

By the time the sun set, we had cooked a quick dinner on the truck's radiator and lain down in the sand to rest. The breakneck pace had exhausted us, and we hoped for a couple hours of sleep before beginning our ascent. Sleep was impossible, however. We knew what lay ahead. It was going to be a rigorous, high-risk operation. Climbing the craggy, scree-covered slope at night would be much more difficult than a daytime venture.

This time there were new obstacles. Half a dozen Bedouin camps were scattered at the base of the mountain. We could hear bleating sheep and barking dogs and see campfires flickering across the valley floor. There were at least two armed sentries guarding the base of the peak. We couldn't figure out why, in two short weeks, the peak had become such a popular gathering place, but these guards significantly raised the stakes. I lay wide awake, listening to the breeze rustling in the scant vegetation and staring at the black-crested peak. It was both beautiful and menacing under its lunar spotlight.

At 10:30 PM Larry rolled over and said, "I can't sleep. Let's just do it."

That was fine with me.

TO THE BRINK

I had a flat-bladed knife strapped to my leg, two bottles of water in my pack, and an itch to get started. I took a deep breath, looked at Larry, and said, "What are we waiting for?"

Our plan was simple. We would use the night-vision binoculars to pick our way across the quarter mile of exposed plain, and then we would make a beeline for the fence. If all went well, we'd dig under the chain link and dash to the safety of the rocks. That would put us within a hundred yards of the archaeological site with its array of pillars and the altar that we could only see from a distance on our last trip. It was a mixed blessing that the moon was now bright enough to read a book by. It could light our way or betray us to our adversaries.

Moving as cautiously as possible, we crossed the valley in spurts. Larry would lead for fifty yards, then I would take over. We could hear every footstep we made in the sand. When we were approximately two hundred yards into the plain—and fully exposed on the flats—the dogs started barking again. First one dog, then two began yapping, and soon there was yelping from everywhere. The quiet night erupted into an ear-splitting cacophony of demonic howls. My blood curdled.

"Do you think they smell us?" Larry whispered. "Can they see us?"

The uproar grew so loud and intense that the dogs seemed to be right on top of us. I pulled out my knife, fully expecting to see dog shadows racing at us from the plain. Larry scrounged a stick to use as a club. I thought about our encounter with the snarling behemoth on the road from Tabuk. This time there would be no car door or window to separate us from the pointed teeth.

There was little doubt that the dogs could smell us. Our only hope was that the Bedouins, thinking we were a rabbit or other animal, would keep the pack tethered. We kept moving toward the fence, trying to block out the noise and shuffling on hands and knees to avoid the sound of footfalls. We were less than forty yards from the fence when Larry's arm shot up.

"Wait!" he whispered, pointing. "There's someone there."

Through the night-vision binoculars, we saw the green-white dot of a lighted cigarette dancing in the dark. A guard or a shepherd was smoking by the fence.

That was very bad news. Digging under the fence was now out of the question. We would have to resort to Plan B, an alternative we had hoped to avoid. It involved soft-stepping another mile north along the exposed plain, dodging sheepdogs and Bedouins in the dark until we reached the end of the fence. From there we would have to climb halfway up the peak and descend to the archaeological site without alerting the guards to our presence. Instead of a quick penetration from ground level to snap a few pictures and beat a hasty retreat to the truck, we now faced the demoralizing prospect of an all-nighter on the precarious slope.

THE CLIMB

The path was arduous and exhausting. Picking our way through the darkness, we were never sure if the next shadow was a bottomless crevasse or a shallow chuckhole. Each step was suspenseful and unsettling. I worried about stepping on an ill-tempered snake or scorpion. We chugged water and gushed sweat. Larry kept the night-vision binoculars glued to his eyes to keep us from tromping through a slumbering shepherds' camp.

It was well after midnight when we finally skirted the fence and began our climb. We had run out of water thirty minutes before and were already afflicted with a ferocious thirst, but we had to press on. We climbed hand over foot, debating every move and painstakingly traversing a diagonal path up the mountain.

It took us another two hours to reach a point where we could look down on the altar. The moon, having changed hues, was now suffusing the mountain in surreal aquamarine sparkles. In that light, the valley floor looked like a giant snowfield. A wind came up, and we shivered in our sweat-soaked shirts. Soon it gusted across the rock face with a menacing howl, throwing dust and biting sand into our faces. We teetered on a narrow ledge feeling exposed and vulnerable. I could just make out the shape of the guardhouse below. Farther south were the ghostly white outlines of the pillar stumps and then the vague, arrowhead-shaped altar.

Shielding my eyes from the stinging sand, I asked Larry, "What are we doing here?" I could see the blue moon reflected in his eyes, the sheen of sweat on his brow.

With a widening grin, he replied, "We're making history, Bob. Making history."

We started down. What had looked like a straight shot from above was actually a maze of ridges and trenches. Descending from our rocky perch, we made two false starts toward the pillars. Scrabbling around in the dark on all fours, we had to go back up the slope, make a new sighting to recalibrate our position, and go back down over rocks and through prickly bushes to the bottom. We communicated with whispers and hand signals, ducking in and out of moon shadows between boulders. We tiptoed past the guardhouse, only to come upon a series of odd stone circles that neither of us had expected.

"Remember David Fasold's letter?" Larry asked. "These must be the stone pillars he found inside the fence."

"Yeah, I remember."

Each structure had three large rings that formed exterior walls two-and-a-half feet thick. They were eighteen feet in diameter, and the twelve of them were spaced five feet apart. Buried at ground level, each circle was filled with dirt. First Fasold and now Larry had called them pillars, but they looked more like ceremonial platforms, or even large cisterns. They lay at the bottom of the ancient riverbed we had seen before, so perhaps they were once water-storage reservoirs for the Hebrew tribes. As he explained in his letter, Fasold had partially excavated one, thinking he would find Hebrew gold or treasure buried inside. Larry and I saw where his crew had dug, but we didn't have the time or tools to investigate further. We took a few pictures, shielding the flash with our hands, and started looking for the altar.

THE PILLARS AND THE V-SHAPED ALTAR

We took our time, moving methodically across the rocky terrain and using the shadows for cover whenever we could. We tried to avoid open, moonlit areas. We finally located the pillar stones, or column fragments, along a makeshift road some thirty yards from the V-shaped altar. There were a dozen of them, smooth to the touch, and hand-chiseled like polished marble. We knew from reading Exodus 24:4 that after receiving the law, Moses got up early in the morning and "built an altar at the foot of the mountain, and twelve pillars according to the twelve tribes of Israel." The pillars we saw fit the description in the Bible; they were close to the altar and at the foot of the mountain. Were these fractured columns the remnants of the twelve pillars erected by Moses and the people of Israel? The prospect was compelling.

"It's like finding fine marble pillars in the Mojave Desert," Larry said. "Something like this doesn't get here by accident."

I agreed. There is always a specific reason for such structures to be where they are. Their size alone, eighteen inches in diameter and twenty-two inches tall, made them a find of some consequence. With growing excitement, we took several close-up photos and moved on toward the altar.

When seen from above, the altar was impressive; up close, it was breathtaking. The large altar was located at the exact foot of the mountain, just as the Bible says, and it was shaped like a giant V. I felt as if I were standing next to an airliner with spread wings, ready for takeoff. We walked its entire length, marveling at this hand-constructed stone formation. It was an anomaly, standing at the base of a mountain in the middle of a desert. Seeing it at close range further cemented our idea that we were examining an ancient foundation, a third of a football field in length. What was it? The Bible states that Moses and the people used it for "burnt offerings," a place where young bulls were sacrificed "as fellowship offerings to the Lord" (Exodus 24:5, NIV).

When we first saw it from an elevated vantage point two weeks earlier, we had seen that its outer stone walls sandwiched an interior wall that ran the length of the V and was parallel to the exterior ramparts. It looked like a corral for penning animals. After we had thoroughly inspected and filmed it, we agreed that it could be the altar described in Exodus.

As we were leaving, I noticed Larry gazing at it with astonishment. Then, as if seeing it for the first time, he said, "This is the altar Moses built, isn't it?"

I looked at the massive structure and knew what Larry was feeling. Moses had touched that wall.

LAST ATTEMPT AT ELIJAH'S CAVE

It was 3:30 AM, and the moon filled the sky. Excitement and wonder had fueled our efforts, but as we pressed on, hiking and climbing, we began to wear down. We were dangerously dehydrated and fatigued from our physical exertions. My body said that it was time to quit, time to make our way back to camp to drink much-needed water and to rest overtired muscles, but the need to quit was less compelling than the urge to continue.

"There's still time to reach Elijah's cave," I said, looking up. I could see it clearly several hundred yards above us. The moonlit hollow gouged into the craggy slope beckoned me. Apparently it was calling Larry with the same siren song.

He took a deep breath. "Here goes nothing."

We began the most dangerous climb of our lives. The slope was already treacherous enough because of its distorted angle and the sometimes confusing moon shadows on the rocks. In our flagging condition, the climb straight up through crumbling rock and talus was madness.

Step-by-step we proceeded, placing one foot and then the next.

The night-vision binoculars were of no use since they were for distance vision. There was no clear path, so we had to muscle our way up through the scree and around jagged overhangs. We were no longer sweating, which was a bad sign of advanced dehydration. My arms and legs felt like petrified stumps.

Step-by-step. First one foot, and then the next.

We struggled on; after nearly an hour, we were seventy yards from the cave and victory was in sight. I just had to worm my way around a sheer rock face.

Then the ground gave way beneath me. The ledge I was standing on wobbled. My footing gave way, and I started sliding backward. I fell hard on my stomach, and the ground moved past me. I was dropping down the near-vertical pitch.

I clawed frantically for a handhold but seized only handfuls of loose gravel. I slid faster toward a blind drop-off that I had avoided earlier. I knew it to be five stories deep. I reached, grabbed, and kicked, trying to sink the toes of my boots into the ground, but I continued to fall.

At the last possible second, as the earth turned to air and launched my bone-breaking death, Larry reached out and clutched my vest. His grip held firm as my legs dangled over the edge. For a moment, all I could hear was my ragged breathing and the kettle-drum beat of my heart.

I painstakingly scratched my way back and regained my footing.

Safe again, I gazed in terrified disbelief at the black maw of the ravine that had almost been my grave.

Larry had saved my life.

We sat for several minutes, gasping air. We both knew that I had almost died, and I was feeling especially mortal and vulnerable. It made me stop and think about what we were doing. The sun was now creeping over the horizon. Soon we'd be climbing in broad daylight for all to see. Our legs felt like wet bags of concrete. We had nothing to drink, and there were still a hundred yards of dangerous cliff above us. I looked at Larry, and we both knew it was over. We weren't going to make it to the cave. My heart, pounding in fear a few moments before, now sank with disappointment.

We dusted ourselves off and started back down. We had accomplished what we had set out to do. We were satisfied with the photos we had taken. I shook off my regret and privately began to celebrate a successful mission.

It felt good to be working with gravity again. We made good time to the bottom and found a hidden draw near the fence that provided a safe exit point. We took another minute to catch our breath and scurried undetected across the valley floor to our truck. We were thankful to find the Bedouin shepherds and guards still asleep in their tents.

When we reached the truck, I unlatched the tailgate, ripped open a box of water, and started gulping. It tasted better than anything I had ever experienced.

"Well," said Larry, splashing handfuls of water on his face and neck. "We did it again."

"Yeah, we did it again," I answered, still out of breath. I looked at the mountain again to say good-bye. It was time to go.

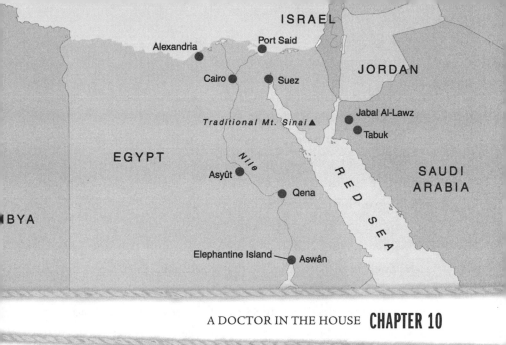

We threw our packs in the pickup bed, devoured some protein bars, and wedged our cramped, waterlogged bodies back into the cab.

As we drove away from the mountain, Larry raised an interesting point. We had followed the Exodus route from Egypt to the tip of Sinai. We had traveled from the crossing site where the Israelites would have come out of the Red Sea along the path to the bitter springs of Marah and then to the seventy palms and twelve springs of Elim. But we hadn't traveled from Al-Bad, where the seventy palms were, across the twenty-eight kilometers through the mountain passes to Jabal al-Lawz. According to Larry, this would make us the first known people since the time of Moses to retrace the entire Exodus route.

"Why not?" I said, smiling. I was in awe at his endless steel will and concrete determination. He had courage to spare. This time I wasn't going to bail on him.

We started on our way, and twenty minutes later we were lost.

Less than half an hour after our departure, our zigzagging over and around the dunes had left us utterly bewildered. Moses had something on his journey through this desert that we didn't have. The Exodus story tells of a pillar of fire and a column of cloud that had guided Moses and the Israelites through the bewildering desert. Such supernatural guidance would have been welcome.

Instead of a fiery pillar, we had only our own sense of direction, which put us at a disadvantage. Out of all the choices we made, I'm convinced that we made the wrong one every time. One wrong valley led to other wrong valleys. That was when we met the Bedouin in his pickup and asked for help. Within the hour, we had been shoved into a sweatbox jail in the middle of the desert.

We were captives.

The minutes passed slowly in the cell. My back ached from sitting on the hard dirt floor, covered only by a worn Persian rug. The heat was still oppressive, the rotting-meat stench still hung in the thick air, and armed men still guarded us, spitting and calling us Jews. The hatred so clear in our guards' eyes contrasted with the innocence of two boys who sat motionless against the far wall of the cell, staring curiously at Larry and me.

"*Gahwah!*" Our red-eyed captor barked the Arabic word over his shoulder. It was a term he had used before, and it made my stomach twist.

"Here we go again," Larry said. The disgust in his voice matched that in my gut, and I could only groan.

Every fifteen minutes, the commander shouted this short

Arabic command, and the boys would hop up and dart to a smoky fire pit by the door. Using steel tongs, they tilted a cast-iron kettle and filled two small, ornate silver cups with a syrupy liquid that tasted like the dregs of a vinegar vat.

"I'm not doing this again," I mumbled to Larry. I had already downed more than I could stomach. The smell of the room had sent nausea roiling through me like waves pounding a beach. Adding the brew to my stomach made things worse.

In a failing attempt to fight off the heat, our bodies were pouring out sweat, fluids we were not replenishing. The few sips of the drink we had forced down were insufficient to compensate for the fluids we had lost. My blurred vision was a sign of dehydration.

The boys brought the cups to us and held them out as if doing us a favor. I looked at the silver cups and then at the boys. The concoction was supercharged Bedouin coffee made from boiled green coffee beans and cardamom seeds, a jolting caffeine concoction they called *gahwah*. If the caffeine didn't keep us alert, the pungent smell certainly would.

"Do you think they'll shoot us if we say no?" I whispered.

Larry shrugged. "They may shoot us anyway."

I raised my hand and shook my head. There was no way I could take another sip of that noxious drink. One of the boys gave me a disappointed look and walked head down and stoop shouldered to the steeping pot and emptied the cup. His companion did the same. They returned to their cross-legged positions across the chamber. I felt sorry for the boys. We had rejected their hospitality. To make amends, I gave them a smile and an appreciative wink. They sat up and returned the smile. These boys had not yet learned to hate, and they didn't appear to despise us as infidels, as non-

Muslims are called. The boys presented a sad, odd image to my Western mind. Their blousy Bedouin robes swallowed their gaunt frames. One of them carried a rusty automatic rifle over his shoulder, the weapon almost as tall as he was. He carried it proudly, an Arab warrior's prop that belied his boyish innocence.

I returned my attention to the commander. He was dressed in military fatigues and boots, most likely a member of the frontier forces assigned to police the vast Saudi desert. He was rubbing his red eye, which apparently had a chunk of desert grit lodged under the lid. When he saw that we weren't drinking, it added to his irritation. He knew that we needed to hydrate in the punishingly hot air, and he seemed, for the moment at least, to be concerned about our not getting enough fluids. He probably wanted to keep us alive just long enough to find out what we were doing in his domain. That his men had spit on us and called us Jews was terrifying. Most Arabs loathe Jews—a hatred that is pounded into them from childhood. For many of these men, the more dead Jews there were, the better. If they thought we were Jewish spies sneaking into territory with military radar tracking stations on nearby mountaintops, then we were in the worst kind of trouble.

The commander motioned for me to take another drink by lifting his cupped hand to his face. "*Gahwah*," he commanded.

I pointed to the steeping coffee and twisted my face. Larry joined the protest, even though we were both craving liquids—anything other than that *gahwah*.

The commander parked himself on the camel saddle in front of us. He reached in his shirt pocket, pulled out a date, and rolled it in his fingers. He stared at us through his good eye as if trying to understand our rejection of his kindness. He popped the whole date into his mouth and gnawed at its brown rind. It was summer, and dates in Saudi Arabia are considered the best then, when they begin to turn from a dark brown to a buttery yellow. Then he stood as if he finally understood. It wasn't that we didn't want to drink; it was that we didn't want to drink that blasted *gahwah*. He marched to one of the walls and lifted a brown camel-stomach bag, the desert version of a canteen, from a peg.

The commander snapped a quick order, and one of the boys hopped up to get him a small glass. Untying a shriveled intestine that dangled from the dried stomach, the commander poured a cloudy liquid into the glass. He handed me the drink. I raised it to the fading light that peaked in through the doorway. The milky substance had several long camel-colored hairs floating in it. My tongue by then was feeling like a piece of tar from a Texas highway, so I held my breath and slogged it down. I had to pluck some hair out of my mouth, but the drink was tolerable. It had a sour, gamy taste. I looked at Larry. We had a new beverage of choice!

Satisfied for the moment, the commander left the room, and I was glad to see him go. I turned my head and squinted through a crack in the mortar of the crumbling jail at the endless fire-baked wilderness. Shimmering waves of translucent heat hovered over the sullen sands. My heart sank. Thoughts of escape percolated like *gahwah* in a pot, but such thoughts were useless. Even if we managed to escape, the heat, dehydration, and exhaustion would soon kill us, providing carrion for the desert scavengers.

To my weary gaze, the landscape seemed to pitch and blur in a nightmare of impending death. From where I sat, it seemed a perfect vision of hell.

My leg began to sting. I looked down and saw an ant making free with my leg. Then I realized he wasn't alone. The Persian carpet crawled with them. The small reddish insects had avoided the midday heat, but were now coming out en masse as the sun slipped low on the horizon. They were all over us. I raised my hand to swat one, when a guard sprinted forward and pressed his rifle barrel against my forehead. My sun-scarred captor shook his head, and a venomous gap-toothed smile split his face. We had to endure those fierce little buggers as they crept under our shirt collars and up our pant legs. I could only squirm and scratch when the guards momentarily looked away.

Larry seemed indifferent to the ants. For that matter, Larry seemed indifferent to being in a desert jail. I think that in his own way he was enjoying the unique experience. For him it was always about the challenge, the gut thrill. His steely determination, mixed with his love of risk and bravado, had made him a young millionaire. That same risk and daring had now gotten us neck-deep in big trouble.

The commander was still missing, and I began to worry about our truck. So far—and I considered this a miracle—the sentries had yet to search our vehicle. A search of the pickup would reveal our cargo of night-vision binoculars, satellite photos, expensive metal-detection equipment, and other documents that could get us shot as spies. For some reason, our desert wardens showed no interest in the truck's contents. We had no interest in military espionage, but our overseers wouldn't believe that.

It was not spying that had lured us to this ancient land that the Bible calls Midian but another kind of prize that had loomed too large in our minds to ignore. I again questioned my sanity. Sitting in this stifling, stinking, ant-infested cell made me wish for home, for the embrace of my wife and the faces of my children.

My despair increased. After hours of watching us, the guards were edgy and began bickering among themselves. To pass the time, they slid shells into their vintage rifles and put the muzzles to our heads.

I held my breath as my captor pulled the trigger.

The hammers dropped.

I tried not to wince when the hammers fell because I saw that they were loading empty shells—at least for now. I wanted to mask my fear, but in my years as a policeman I had seen the nasty results of a rifle shot to the head. I tightened every time metal struck metal.

When the guards had finished their game of Terrorize the Prisoners, I leaned back against the wall, frayed, exhausted, and sick with fear. I felt light-headed, as if my heart were pumping syrup to my brain. I was succumbing to thoughts of the grim realities that likely awaited us. We had endured a grueling day of heat, abuse, threats, taunts, foul-tasting drink, and carnivorous ants. It was time to do something, but what? I had churned over every idea I could muster, and all of them seemed destined to unpleasant, perhaps fatal, ends. I glanced at Larry and saw it—the look. Without words being spoken, I knew he had an idea. What I didn't know was whether it was a good idea.

Larry had just received another verbal assault, but this time the guards seemed to be gearing up for something far more physical. Larry leaned his head in my direction and whispered, "I think they're going to kill us. We need to do something, and we need to do it soon."

"Do you have anything in mind?" I whispered back.

He paused, studied me, and glanced at the guard. From the corner of his mouth, he said, "Pretend you're a doctor."

"What? How am I supposed to do that?"

Larry raised a hand, pointed at me, and said loudly, "Doctor. He's a doctor."

I don't know what shocked me most—his willingness to plunge into the plan or his ability to fabricate with a straight face.

The room went silent. Every guard stopped and looked at me. Across the room, the surly, red-eyed commander had returned and was looking me over. "Dooktar?" he mumbled, holstering his pistol.

Clearing a path through the other guards, he marched to me, bent down, and pressed his scowling bearded face close to mine. He raised his hand, and I steeled myself for a blow. Instead, he pointed to his puffy, irritated eye. He pried his lids apart. It was blood-red and watery. Apparently a grain of sand was embedded under his eyelid and had inflamed the normally white sclera of his eyeball. The guards, now engrossed in the drama, put down their rifles.

Everyone, including Larry, waited to see what the doctor would do. I sat frozen for a moment. The commander kept his finger pointing at his eye, slowly saying, "Dooktar," so I would be sure to understand him.

I turned to Larry, who sat expressionless. "What do I do?"

Larry was matter-of-fact. "I don't know; you're the doctor." I waited for him to laugh, and in any other circumstance he might have done just that.

I had to play along. "I need my shave kit from the truck."

Larry saw where I was going and stood. He motioned toward the door and our vehicle. "Supplies. Supplies." A guard stuck a rifle in his face and ordered him to sit down. I appealed to the commander, pointing to his seeping eye and then to the truck. He reluctantly agreed to let me go to it, with an armed escort, of course. I got my black leather shave kit from the back and returned to the dreary cell, where the commander stood waiting. I am sure he was worrying about whether his treatment might hurt just a little or whether the new doctor might need to carve out his eyeball.

I dug around in my bag. The commander stood there fidgeting like an anxious child as he waited for me to tend to his malady. I found a plastic bottle of Visine in the bottom of the bag. I gestured to the commander to tilt his head back, and he complied. I squirted half a bottle of cool liquid into his eye. He blinked and pulled back in reaction to the drops, then stood there smiling broadly. The Visine had soothed his tender eye.

A few minutes later the other guards began jabbering and pointing to their commander's eye. The red of the eye was turning white. I was an instant hit and probably the first "doctor" to visit these parts.

The guards lined up for treatment. There are no pharmacies in the desert. They don't even have toothbrushes, so they break off twigs and rub them over their teeth. The first guard in line complained of a bad cough. Larry stepped in to offer his advice. Larry pointed to the man's cigarettes and shook his head no. The guard scowled at Larry—and rightfully so. After all, I was the doctor!

I smiled and nodded a reassuring okay, while pointing to his cigarettes. The man grinned and turned his nose up at Larry, who sat back down and offered no more help.

A physician friend had given me medicine before we left for Saudi. He had donated several samples of prescription drugs for use in unforeseen circumstances, including pills for pain and infection. He had even included sleeping pills. That got me to thinking. Sleeping pills! So I gave the guy five sleeping pills—one for each guard. He bowed an appreciative thank you, then threw all five pills in his mouth, chewing the sour tablets like candy.

Larry raised his eyebrows and smiled. "Good plan!"

All the guards, including the commander, were soon crunching away on the sleeping pills. Within twenty minutes, the pills kicked in. Some of the Bedouins started to fidget, then nod. Some yawned, while others searched for a cozy spot to nap. The commander tossed a camel's saddle on the dirt floor for a pillow and covered it with a wool blanket. Two others leaned against the concrete wall.

Then they slept—all, that is, except for the young man standing guard just outside. We watched closely as he began murmuring to himself, pacing nervously and trying to shake his comrades awake. No one moved, which heightened his alarm. He started waving his pistol threateningly in our direction.

Pistol or not, Larry and I realized that this was probably our only chance to escape. We knew that if we waited around, the others would wake up, and we would be in worse shape than ever. We'd never get out alive. With the guard agitated and distracted by his friends, we quietly put on our shoes and socks. Then, smiling and offering a few friendly nods, we walked from the cellblock toward the truck. The guard stopped what he was doing and followed us, waving his pistol in our direction. We remained calm and bowed politely. I noticed in his manner a youthful indecision and a reluctance to use the gun. With his sidekicks snoring in the dirt, he seemed lost.

As we continued to the truck, I noticed that I was holding my breath. I opened the door, took my seat, turned the key, and gave the engine some gas. Larry took the other seat. We were about to drive off when the young sentry flew into a rage. He screamed at the top of his lungs and ran in front of our truck, pointing his pistol at Larry's head. I expected him to shoot us both.

Instead of shooting, he motioned with his pistol for us to stay put. He called for one of the younger boys standing nearby, and they hopped into a green, military-looking pickup parked not far from ours. With a wave of his arm and a loud shout in Arabic, the frontier guard ordered us to follow him. He popped the clutch and sped away into the wilderness. We raced across the desert floor close behind our livid young jailer, heading straight toward the town of Tabuk.

While buying supplies in Tabuk prior to our illegal foray into the desert, I had heard from a Muslim merchant that two Americans were being held in the Tabuk prison for preaching from the Bible. I also heard that they had beheaded an eighteen-year-old American who had smuggled cocaine into Saudi Arabia.

The spinning tires of the truck ahead of us whipped up a cloud of dust so thick I could hardly make out the road. I slowed down to get a little distance, and the young guard slammed on his brakes, skidding to a stop. I almost rear-ended him. He leapt from the truck, ran back, and pointed his gun at my temple. Then, with wild shouts and threatening gestures, he rapped the pistol barrel on the speedometer as if to say, "Hurry up! Hurry up!" The message was clear.

We barreled overland without path or trail at out-of-control speeds. We rammed into fat dunes, clattered across rock-strewn gullies, and bottomed out over brush-covered ridges, finally leveling out into a vast red-hued valley with a long, smooth plain. Reddish dirt covered Larry's face and hair. Even his teeth were brown from inhaling the choking dust. I was sure I looked the same.

Larry looked over at me and shouted, "We need to get rid of the stuff in the back of the pickup. It's evidence we don't want with us."

"How?"

"Slow down, only this time, easy does it. Slow down gradually."

"Got it."

Over the next ten miles, I gradually reduced my speed until there was a little distance between us and the truck in front. I kept the pickup in the dust cloud, hoping it would hide our actions.

"I don't think he can see what we're doing," I shouted. "Go! Quick! We don't have much time."

We bounced along at sixty miles an hour on a dirt-packed road. Larry pulled himself out the window, then slid his leg out and over onto the rear railing. Somehow he climbed into the bed of the pickup. Larry wasted no time in tossing out the incriminating evidence—film, infrared binoculars, satellite photos, topographical maps of Jabal al-Lawz, area maps, shovels, and even our compass and thermometer. The thought of what we were leaving behind sickened me.

Larry had emptied almost everything from the bed of the battered pickup. I leaned over and opened the door, and in perfect form, Larry grabbed it and swung his legs and torso back inside the cab, absorbing several punishing body shots from the lurching chassis.

"You have another job to do," I said. "Take the grill off the air vent in the dashboard and hide a roll of film in there."

"What? Why—"

"Just do it. Trust me on this." I closed the distance between the trucks, hoping to avoid another outburst from the pistol-wielding guard. Larry managed to remove the air vent. "Open your duffel bag and take out a pair of socks—black socks, if you have them."

He did but not until he had given me a look that told me he was questioning my sanity.

"Now what?" he asked.

"Put the film in the sock and the sock in the vent, then replace the cover."

Again, he did as I instructed. Once the vent cover was in place, he leaned back. "I can barely see the sock. If I didn't know it was there..."

"You wouldn't see it," I said, finishing his sentence. "It's an old drug smuggler's trick. I came across it a few times when I was a cop."

That trick gave me one thing to feel good about, but I was heartsick about what we had left behind in our dust. All the work, all the risk, and we had unceremoniously tossed it into the desert. No one would ever see it.

With a little more time and better circumstances, we might have hidden more film, but at that moment it was enough to get one roll. We had other things on our minds, such as somehow getting out of this mess alive.

We pulled into Tabuk, and the young guard stopped at a T-intersection in front of a high-walled cement prison rimmed with curls of barbed wire and guard towers. My stomach dropped like an elevator with severed cables. The sight of the building sent chills down my spine.

As the truck idled at the stop sign, I swallowed hard, forcing down a wad of choking dust lodged in my throat.

"You don't think ...," I began.

"I hope not," Larry said, looking at the barbed wire on the wall. Then, "He's moving."

I breathed a sigh of relief when the guard steered away from the prison and drove down the main street. He led us to a few police stations, but they were closed. The police were probably sleeping or at prayers.

At every police station it was the same. Our young guard would knock, and no one would answer. It would have been comical if I hadn't been scared spitless. At one station, a young boy of about fourteen answered the door as if he were the chief of police. He scowled and led us to a holding cell that had a few throw pillows and a wobbling ceiling fan that creaked at each revolution. There was no air-conditioning; the heat was just as bad as in the desert cell, and the foul drink still stank.

Several other officers arrived and listened to our captor's impassioned story, occasionally casting dark glances our way. After some time and frequent requests, the desert guard allowed us to use the phone. Larry called the car-rental place and told them what was happening and he also called our hotel. The manager invited everyone over to the hotel to have a cool drink and calm down. Larry's big tipping was apparently returning some residuals.

Without knowing the details of the phone discussions between the police and the manager, it was difficult to unscramble what was happening, but we were soon standing in the hotel manager's office at the Tabuk Sahara. It was there that Larry ran out of patience. We had been up for three nights; we were hungry and growing testy. Our stress had reached the breaking point, and Larry blew up. He pulled out the forged letter we had used to get our visas for our first trip and slammed it face up on the table.

I couldn't believe my eyes. Why would he bring that incriminating piece of evidence with him? It was a gutsy and dangerous move that could get our heads lopped off. Larry was hoping that it would get us out.

That false letter sat on the wooden table. My stomach clenched, and my heart stuttered. Larry didn't blink; he demanded that they release us and that they do so immediately. After all, we were honored guests of the royal family. The hotel manager read the letter aloud in Arabic.

With an abruptness that startled even the hotel manager, one of the policemen placed our passports, cameras, and keys on the table, then announced, "We will check out your story."

The hotel manager cringed as he translated for us.

He ordered us to stay put in that hotel until the police released us. We were under house arrest, and the officers left.

So did we.

A few hours later we boarded a flight to King Kahlid International Airport. After a gut-tightening layover in Riyadh, we were finally on a jet heading for New York City.

As I dropped into a deep, peaceful sleep, my last thought was that I had once again stood on holy ground. I understood how Jim Irwin must have felt on the moon when he saw the handiwork of God stretched across the universe. I had seen monuments to the Exodus story that had lain undisturbed in the sands of Midian for more than three thousand years, and now I believed—I believed it all.

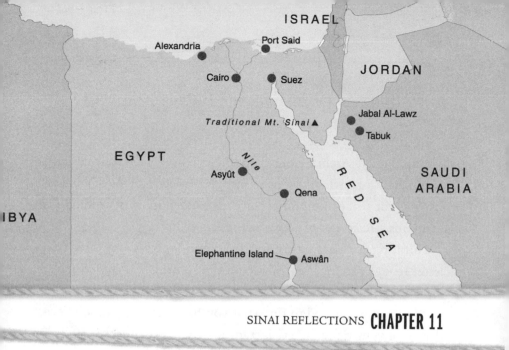

Over the next few months, Larry and I tried to get back into the rhythm of our regular lives. He returned to trading commodities and running marathons—and I even heard a rumor that he had gone to the desert somewhere in New Mexico to look for a cache of Spanish gold in an old mine shaft. I went back to working with Jim Irwin as vice president of his High Flight Foundation and running a real estate company with my brother.

Soon, day-to-day realities eclipsed our crazy adventures in the sweltering Saudi desert, but I would never forget my time with Larry Williams. What a great guy! He would be drenched in sweat, looking half dead, yet with a twinkle in his eye he would say, "Hey, Bob, what's over there beyond that far-off ridge?" I knew I couldn't take one more agonizing step, but Larry would head off toward the horizon, and I would soon muster the strength to follow.

In the years to come, I would learn more about the evidence for Mount Sinai in Arabia. Not surprisingly, I discovered that a wealth of information—which overwhelmingly leaned in favor of Jabal al-Lawz as the real Mount Sinai—already existed in musty old books in an obscure corner of a nearby university library.

Not long after our return to the United States, Larry received a letter from a foremost authority on the subject of Mount Sinai, a Jewish scholar named Allen Kerkeslager, who wrote:

"You will be pleased to find that you have some good, solid evidence for your views. A Jewish tradition dating to at least 250 BCE . . . identified Mount Sinai with the highest mountain near ancient Madyan, which is the modern town of Al-Bad. The most likely candidate, I have concluded, is Jabal al-Lawz. As far as I know, this is currently the most elaborate scholarly treatment of the evidence that would support an identification of Mount Sinai with Jabal al-Lawz."

According to Dr. Kerkeslager, "The earliest solid date for the appearance of traditions locating Mount Sinai in the southern Sinai Peninsula is ca. 350 AD."[3] Citing ancient Jewish historians such as Josephus, Kerkeslager insists that in identifying the real Mount Sinai, three considerations must be taken into account: the mountain must be in northwestern Arabia, it must be near Al-Bad (ancient Madyan), and it must be the highest mountain in the surrounding region.

Jabal al-Lawz is clearly the tallest mountain in northwest Arabia, and no other mountain better fits Dr. Kerkeslager's premise for the real Mount Sinai.

I was sent a voluminous doctoral dissertation on the location of

Mount Sinai in Saudi Arabia by a Dr. Chuck Whittaker. He concluded that "with the many varied arguments . . . demonstrating the biblical significance of Jabal al-Lawz, this site in Saudi Arabia remains the best candidate for Mount Sinai/Horeb."

In *Bible Review,* Dr. Frank Moore Cross, professor emeritus at Harvard University, claims that "a reasonable guess for the identity of Mount Sinai is Jabal al-Lawz."

I also learned that a host of ancient historians pointed to either Arabia as the location for Mount Sinai or to Jabal al-Lawz directly as the real Mount Sinai. Philo of Alexandria (13 BC–AD 45) points to Arabia as the traditional location of Mount Sinai. Eusebius (ca. 260–339) locates "the mountain of God" in "the outlying countryside of Madiam." He also locates Madiam (Madyan) itself "toward the desert of the Saracens on the east of the Red Sea." Jerome (ca. 347–419) locates Mount Sinai (Horeb) "with a location near Madyan in northwestern Arabia east of the Red Sea." And the Jewish historian Josephus (ca. 37–100) pointed directly to the highest mountain in that region of Saudi Arabia, which would be Jabal al-Lawz, as the real Mount Sinai.

While such information supports my belief that Jabal al-Lawz is the true Mount Sinai, there is something else to consider. I have traveled to the site twice, enduring hardship and risking arrest and imprisonment to prove a point, but the point may have proven me. During my first trip up the mountain, I was overwhelmed with the idea that I was standing on ground that was once too holy to touch. Perhaps it still was.

THE SPLIT ROCK

One of the most amazing finds about Jabal al-Lawz came from a fascinating couple named Jim and Penny Caldwell. In early December 1991, after our Saudi Arabian adventures, the Gulf War had recently ended, and the region had once again settled. Jim Caldwell was working for an American oil company in Saudi Arabia, and he and his family lived in the country. Saudi regulations required that they leave the kingdom for one month every year, so they decided to take a family vacation to Egypt. They visited many of the tourist spots, including the traditional Mount Sinai at Saint Catherine's Monastery, the same place I had visited with Jim Irwin a few years before. Their assessment of the site was the same as ours. It was a huge disappointment for them, as it was obvious that the mountain in Egypt was not the Mount Sinai of the Bible.

Seemingly by chance, while visiting a tiny shop in the resort town of Sharm al-Sheikh, they came across a lone book shelved in the back of the store. It was titled *The Gold Mines of Midian*. Written by Sir Richard Burton in the 1800s, the book contained a map showing Midian as located in northwest Saudi Arabia. As students of the Bible, they knew that Midian was where Moses was tending Jethro's flocks at Mount Sinai, and Midian was also the ancient land where they now lived. They vowed to find the true Mountain of God.

After learning that others had been to a mountain called Jabal al-Lawz and found amazing things there, they made plans to go to the mountain. Since they were Saudi residents, they were able to obtain travel permits. They went to Tabuk and headed across the desert. Guards still patrolled the fence, guarding the front of Jabal al-Lawz, so they used extreme caution as they filmed while hiding in the rocks and gullies. While driving around the backside of the mountain, trying to find a way to hike in safely, they became lost in a maze of wadis.

Traveling over sand and rocks, they entered a valley and saw something that took their breath away. A massive, four-story rock was perched on top of a hill, split down its middle. They also found evidence that water had once flowed from its base. The region only gets about half an inch of rain every ten years. The granite rocks were worn smooth below the split, and there was evidence that long, dry waterfalls were carved into the landscape below. Jim and Penny knew that Scripture spoke of an enormous volume of water surging from the rock at Horeb. "He split open the rocks in the wilderness to give them water, as from a gushing spring. He made streams pour from the rock, making the waters flow down like a river!" (Psalm 78:15-16, NLT). "He split open a rock, and water gushed out to form a river through the dry wasteland" (Psalm 105:41, NLT).

The Bible reveals that after crossing the Red Sea, the Israelites spent several days in the desert, where they became weary from thirst. Quarreling with Moses, they demanded, "Give us water to drink."

In a fit of despair, Moses pleaded with God, "What shall I do with this people? They are almost ready to stone me!" God answered that Moses was to take his staff and strike a particular rock, "and water will come out of it, that the people may drink" (Exodus 17:4-6).

When Moses struck the rock at Horeb (Mount Sinai), it split in two and water erupted like a great geyser, cascading down the hill. Jim and Penny saw a massive rock cloven in two, just as the Bible describes. The extreme erosion in the area was not from wind but was more likely due to an enormous volume of water coming from the split in that giant rock.

FINAL THOUGHTS ON SINAI

The discoveries that Larry and I made, along with those of the Caldwells and others, make a compelling case that Jabal al-Lawz is the real Mount Sinai. History is a one-time event. No one can repli-cate a historical event as if it were a scientific experiment. All any-one has is reliable testimony and gathered evidence. That is not a weakness. There is enough evidence to demonstrate that Jabal al-Lawz is the most likely candidate for being Mount Sinai, and I per-sonally believe it is the true Mountain of God.

Some are not interested in facts to help them make a decision about the past—especially about the Bible as history; they only want confirmation from others to justify an opinion already held. For these people, no amount of evidence will ever be enough. Some, on the other hand, say that all we need is faith. For those who have this gift, it is a blessing; but in the hundreds of talks I have given around the world, I have seen people in the coils of doubt and confusion.

In our culture there are those who want and need evidence, but they are skeptical of any new discovery or sensational claim. After the crucifixion of Jesus, Thomas was confused and questioned the claim that Christ was again alive. Thomas said he needed to see and touch the scars on Christ's body to believe. Jesus met him a week later and showed him the wounds in his side and hands, and after seeing the evidence, Thomas fell to his knees and exclaimed, "My Lord and my God!" (John 20:28, NLT).

I relate to Thomas. I'm an evidence man. Maybe it's because of my upbringing or because of years as a police investigator. Or maybe it's just my nature. I can't blame Thomas for wanting a little more evidence. I traveled around the world to look for a mountain and found it.

I found something else: I found a new level of belief and I found myself.

Words from the Exodus sum it up: "Did any people ever hear the voice of God speaking out of the midst of the fire, as you have heard, and live? Or did God ever try to go and take for Himself a nation from the midst of another nation, by trials, by signs, by wonders, by war, by a mighty hand and an outstretched arm, and by great terrors, according to all that the Lord your God did for you in Egypt before your eyes? To you it was shown, that you might know that the Lord Himself is God; there is none other besides Him" (Deuteronomy 4:33-35).

But there's more. . . .

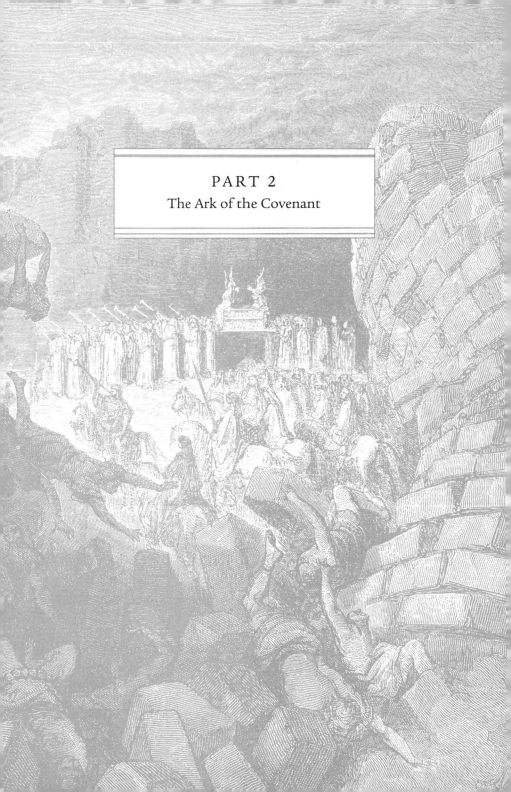

PART 2
The Ark of the Covenant

California, 1991

"Jim Irwin died."

These three words over the phone left me feeling numb. Jim was my friend, my mentor, my inspiration. Now he was gone, and the news ripped a gaping hole in my heart.

Three days later I was flying to Colorado Springs to attend the memorial service. With me was astronaut Buzz Aldrin. Jim had suffered a heart attack on a demanding bike ride in the mountains of Colorado. Of the twelve men who walked on the moon, he was the first to die.

Heroes aren't supposed to die. We know they do, but it never seems right or fair. Men who travel through space and walk on the moon seem invulnerable, but they die like the rest of us. It was a hard truth and one that I didn't want to accept. No denials, however, would change the reality.

Five of the Apollo astronauts attended Jim's funeral. I couldn't help watching them and wondering what they were thinking as they stared at the casket resting in the front of the church. These men belonged in the select fraternity of those who allowed themselves to be stuffed into a small capsule perched atop a hissing, 360-foot Saturn rocket. They had heard the hatch close like a dungeon door, sealing them inside. And then the electrifying word *ignition* poured into their helmets. The massive missile shuddered and roared to life in a flaming ball of indescribable fury that lifted the metal monster skyward, spaceward, moonward. Jim had told me that the force of the liftoff built to 4 g's, plastering him into his seat. They had departed the earth then, and now Jim had departed in another way.

What were these historical icons thinking as they gazed at the coffin that held their comrade? Someday they would take the same voyage from this life as Jim had—a journey beyond the bounds of earth into the unfathomable beyond. Were they preparing for that final journey with the same amount of time, education, zeal, and planning as they had for their trip to the moon?

However heroic our past, the same fate awaits us. I couldn't know what they were thinking, but I knew what I was thinking: Jim had just gone where I would go someday.

I had several talks with Mary Irwin after her husband's death. One day, she looked me in the eye and said, "You must take the flag that has fallen at Jim's passing. Go and find the evidence that a doubting world needs."

I wasn't sure how to respond.

She added, "God didn't have you go off and find the real Mount Sinai for nothing."

I had come to believe that I would probably never return to Saudi Arabia. I figured that Jim's death had ended an exciting era of biblical explorations. He was the man, the catalyst, the spark for us all. Without Jim, some light was turned off, and the book on my biblical explorations was closed.

Mary knew that Jim's passing had siphoned the inspiration out of me and the others who were involved with his work. She made a simple but profound suggestion. "Don't do anything now. Don't make any decision yet. Just pray about it. Don't say no or set off headlong trying to find lost fragments of biblical history." She paused, then whispered, "If it's meant to be, then you won't find the opportunity to continue Jim's work—the opportunity will find you."

I did what she said. I prayed and nothing happened. There was no hint of a divine nod or even an internal smoldering, just empty silence. I drifted away from any notion of further adventures in biblical discovery.

GRAND HAVEN, MICHIGAN

Two years later, in 1993, my wife, Terry, and I drove down an icy road into a dense, snowy thicket, arriving at the entrance to an estate guarded by an enormous gate. I eased from the car, walked to the intercom box, and pressed the call button.

"Hello?" said a voice.

"I'm Robert Cornuke. I'm here to see Robert Van Kampen."

Immediately the gate swung open. We drove another mile or so along a winding lane, through rolling hills in a snow-frosted forest.

Finally, we passed frozen dunes that angled sharply against Lake Michigan's barren shoreline and arrived at a handsome beach house perched on a crusty knoll overlooking the shore. From the car, we could see a tall dead stand of Indian grass and bushy pines shivering under the bitter lakefront wind. We wrapped up tight and went to the front door. Robert Van Kampen opened it himself.

Robert Van Kampen was a billionaire who fit the mold of an old-style baron philanthropist. His father had amassed a fortune in brick manufacturing, and young Robert had made his reputation selling bonds, eventually founding a pioneering investment firm. When he sold Van Kampen Funds to Xerox in 1984, he netted $200 million. Today, the company controls more than $79 billion in assets.

Van Kampen had a reputation for getting to the point. I had the feeling that if it hadn't been for his wife, Judy, he would have quickly dragged me aside and started grilling me with questions. We had dinner and then spent some time getting acquainted with our hosts in their living room. I wasn't sure why Terry and I had been asked to fly to Michigan and was eager to find out, but first I had to ask if Van Kampen would show me his famous 1456 Gutenberg Bible.

"I don't see why not." He strolled from the room and returned a few minutes later, carrying a large, leather-bound Bible held together with metal hinges that made me think of a castle door. The ornate binding had a medieval look and texture. Handing it carefully to me he said, "It contains the book of Daniel from an original Gutenberg Bible."

I was holding one of the oldest and rarest printing-press manuscripts in history, and I savored every second. Terry reached over and skimmed her fingertips lightly across the aged parchment. "These pages feel so . . . old," she said.

Van Kampen stiffened. "You might want to be careful with those," he said. "Each page is worth over thirty thousand dollars."

"No!" Terry shot back. "Do you mind if I have this one?" She took a playful swipe at the page, pretending to rip it out. Van Kampen didn't see the humor. He took the Bible and closed it.

"It's late," he said, and stood. "Let's continue our conversation in the morning." A few minutes later, we were in the guest room.

The morning light strained through the gloomy clouds that hovered over Lake Michigan. Terry and I joined the Van Kampens for morning coffee.

"May I speak with you privately?" Van Kampen asked me.

"Certainly." We excused ourselves, leaving our wives chatting in the breakfast nook. He led me to his personal office and wasted no time getting down to business.

"You were vice president of Jim Irwin's ministry, and that's all I need to know. Would you consider heading up my ministry?" I must have looked as confused as I felt because he added, "I'm talking about my collection of manuscripts and Bibles. I'd like you to oversee it all."

My mouth went dry. His collection is one of the world's great biblical research resources.

"Thank you. I'm honored to be considered for such a position," I said, "but I'll have to give it some serious consideration."

Van Kampen glared at me, as if to say, *How dare you trivialize my offer by saying you'll have to think about it!*

I rallied, "Mr. Van Kampen, it's a very attractive offer, and aspects of the job genuinely appeal to me. But I'll need to go home, discuss it with Terry, and take a few weeks before I can give you an answer."

Van Kampen gave a confused nod and strode over to a bookcase. He grabbed a volume and handed it to me. It was *The Sign and the Seal* by Graham Hancock. Judging from the cover, I could see it had something to do with the Ark of the Covenant.

"I'd like you to read this and tell me what you think. I found it a fairly clever account of the search for the Ark of the Covenant. Tell me if you think the writer is credible."

I glanced again at the cover and thumbed through some pages. "I've never heard of this," I admitted. "I'll be happy to look it over."

I tucked it under my arm, and we returned to our wives. After breakfast, Terry and I said good-bye and left to catch our afternoon flight. We drove back through the snowy dunes and timbers, and out the front gate.

I never saw Van Kampen again. Some weeks later, I called and formally declined his offer. Terry and I had agreed that uprooting our lives in Colorado to move to Michigan wasn't the best for our family. Informed of my decision, Van Kampen thanked me for my time and wished me well. Not long after our trip to Grand Haven, Van Kampen contracted a rare viral disease that slowly destroyed his heart. He died in November 1999 at the age of sixty, waiting for a heart transplant.

INTERESTED . . . BUT NOT YET

I immediately read the book Van Kampen had given me. Hancock is a noted journalist and investigator, but he is far from being a biblical scholar. In his book he questions the present-day location of the Ark of the Covenant and theorizes so far outside traditional paradigms that most scholars either dismiss his thesis or show little interest. Some thought it had some merit.

Hancock's six hundred-page book traces the Ark of the Covenant from Solomon's Temple to Ethiopia. The Ethiopians claim that they still have it. The book's numbing details make it hard to read, but the author's unique investigative journalism pulled me along, and I came to appreciate his exhaustive work.

Could the Ark of the Covenant actually be in modern Ethiopia? At first I dismissed the idea, yet as I waded deeper into *The Sign and the Seal,* my investigative mind softened to the amazing ideas Hancock proposed. A body of historical evidence emerged from his years of relentless research in Ethiopia, which seemed to cut a swath through layers of muddled traditions. His arguments gave some historical credibility to the idea that the holy box is in Ethiopia today. After finishing the book, I was intrigued, but the only action I took was to place it alongside the other volumes in my bookcase. I moved on to other pressing business, but a seed had been planted that would sprout five years later.

THE ROAD TO ETHIOPIA **CHAPTER 13**

Little Rock, Arkansas, 1998

Five years had passed since I shelved Graham Hancock's book. I was in Little Rock on business and having dinner with friends, Dr. Lindy Book and her husband, Joby. The conversation that night somehow turned to the Ark of the Covenant and Ethiopia. I told them about Hancock's book and how he proposed that the Ark of the Covenant was in Ethiopia. I was stunned when, minutes into our conversation, Dr. Lindy wrote out a check to cover expenses for a research trip. As she pressed the check into my hand, she said with a wink and a smile, "Take Joby with you; he needs a little adventure. Go see if your Ark is in Ethiopia."

This spontaneous donation sent me down a misty path in a far-off place. I was about to enter a realm of mysterious monks and priests who called themselves the "keepers of the Ark."

ADDIS ABABA, ETHIOPIA

In March 1998, Joby and I took a flight to Addis Ababa, Ethiopia.

The first rays of dawn cast a dull pink light through the plane's window as we descended into a world where palm-thatched huts melded with the third-world metropolis that is the capital of Ethiopia. Joby stared out the window, taking it all in. Born in Louisiana, reared in Houston, and living in Arkansas, Joby is a lanky good ol' boy who somehow manages to insert his favorite expression, "Hey, Bubba!" into every third or fourth sentence.

After clearing customs, we walked out of the terminal to see an old-model compact car that had been painted a bright yellow. Apparently the paint job had come out of a spray can because globs of paint streaked the sides of the car. Someone had screwed a wooden sign to the top that read TAKSI.

The driver hopped out, eagerly opened the door to his cab, and chirped, "Where to go, misters?"

"Hotel," Joby answered, and the driver sped us down the road toward the city.

We passed wooded hillsides and gullies cut with muddy streams. Filthy ghettos featured crippled beggars and panhandling children. Prostitution and AIDS run rampant in Addis, where skilled workers earn two dollars a day. Swarms of sickly children have little to eat and only rudimentary medical care. Addis Ababa is a metaphor for Africa as a whole.

The driver took us to a dreary, dirty hotel, but we were too exhausted from the long flight to seek better accommodations. The next morning came none too soon. We were happy to check out of the Cockroach Inn and catch our commuter flight to the northern city of Aksum, where Ethiopians claim to keep the Ark of the Covenant.

The small twin-prop Fokker 50 flew us across a brown, deeply furrowed countryside into endless miles of gritty hills and desolate canyons. From the air, the land looked wild and inhospitable. As we traveled farther north, the countryside became a prairie of red clay, painted bluffs, and angular arroyos—a chalk-dry wasteland quilted with patches of primitive green fieldwork.

As Aksum came into view, our pilot throttled back the engines and began a steep, banking descent. Swooping out of the sky at a nearly vertical pitch, our plane leveled just in time to buzz scores of shepherds, sending their flocks scurrying for cover. As we arced skyward, I looked down to see several men in filthy white robes shooing grazing cows and camels out of the way with long sticks. That was when I realized that the pasture below was our landing strip.

I held my breath as the pilot took a second pass at the runway, this time dropping down and hitting the hard ground, sending rocks and debris up onto the wings and pelting the plane's under-carriage. The plane shuddered down a washboard runway, braking to a stop in a swirl of dust only a few yards from a barbed-wire fence.

I turned to see Joby's white face. I smiled and tried to hide my own perspiring neck and forehead. The thought of touching down on such primitive surfaces seemed suicidal, yet these gutsy Ethiopian Airlines pilots did it every day.

Joby and I gathered ourselves and our bags and stepped into the blinding sunshine. With a few Aksumites lugging bulky canvas bundles on their shoulders, we clambered down the steps to the most primitive, ramshackle airport I have ever encountered. Burned-out, bullet-riddled military planes, trucks, and assorted chunks of battlefield refuse were strewn about. Mangy sheep nibbled at stalks of grass growing through shrapnel holes in rusted metal carcasses. Since the early 1990s, Aksum had been locked in bloody guerrilla warfare. The conflict had decimated the countryside, and many graves peppered the surrounding hill.

The airport terminal was a knobby frame of wooden poles lashed together by wire; sheets of corrugated tin had been nailed to poles and rafters to form crude walls and a roof. Beams of sunlight bled through yawning gaps in the ill-fitting panels. A hand-painted sign hanging on a rusty nail told us we had reached the Aksum terminal, a leaky structure no more than thirty by twenty feet.

As we crossed the pasture to retrieve our luggage, we passed a bearded old man in a ratty robe sitting on a stool by the front door.

"Look at that," Joby said.

He pointed to a spot behind the old man. There, quivering in the shadows, swarmed thousands of bees, flowing in and out of a large hive perched high on a wall inside the dilapidated terminal. The drone of rushing wings unsettled the otherwise quiet noontime air. The bees crawled over the man, head to foot, covering his ears, neck, and beard. Amazingly, the old fellow, seemingly unconcerned, paid the bees no mind.

I heard the roar of an engine and turned to see our plane clatter off, its prop wash blowing Joby's hat from his head and sending it cartwheeling down the rutted dirt path. Down the runway, two men chased some straggling goats out of the way just in time. The plane lifted off, making a steep, sweeping pass over the red-brown cliffs.

That's when the flies hit. Buzzing, stinging flies targeted our

mouths, eyes, and noses. From that moment, they waged a relentless assault. Piles of animal dung lay everywhere, and I quickly recalled that we had landed in a part of Ethiopia that had endured
endless cycles of famine and disease. Our feeling of isolation un-
nerved us. We stood silently for several minutes, listening as our
plane's droning engines faded into the southern horizon.

Joby broke the silence. "Welcome to the end of the world,
Bubba."

For Joby, it was the end of the world—but in spite of the flies, the
bees, and the dilapidated terminal, I soon warmed to the idea of being on an adventure in the rugged heart of Africa.

Soon a young man in his early twenties strode up out of nowhere. "Hello," he said in clear English. "I am Ecuba. I would be
honored to serve as your guide." Ecuba had a big toothy grin and
a shiny dark face; he wore a T-shirt, sandals, and faded Levis. "If
you come with me," he continued, "I will take you to get food and
water."

"Ecuba, huh?" I looked him over, then scanned our present sur-
roundings. He seemed nice enough, and we certainly didn't know
anyone else in Aksum. "All right. Is there a hotel in town?"

"Yes," he said with a nod. "There is a hotel that will accommodate you. I work there."

"How much?" I asked, but Joby jerked my arm.

"I don't care what it costs," he whispered through clenched
teeth. "Pay him the money."

Before I could even negotiate a rate, Joby put his hand on
Ecuba's shoulder and squeezed firmly. "Just take us to the hotel,"
he said, and reached for his wallet. "We'll pay whatever you ask, no
matter how much!"

DUSTY KINGDOM

Aksum is little more than a dusty village decaying into obscurity. At the center of this town sits a simple, thick-walled chapel known as Saint Mary of Zion Church. Ethiopians claim that this humble structure holds the greatest secret in history. From the lowliest peasant to the highest public official, all Ethiopians insist that the Ark of the Covenant rests securely within Saint Mary of Zion's fortified inner sanctum. No one else on earth makes such a claim.

Ethiopians also maintain that no one will ever see the Ark of the Covenant except for one man—the Guardian of the Ark. The Guardian is a spiritual man selected from the priests and assigned to spend his entire life in worshipful solitude, guarding the Ark. He will never leave the small fenced chapel of Saint Mary of Zion Church until he is carried away for his funeral.

We passed a bizarre pageant of humanity en route to the hotel. It was market day, and men, women, and children choked the street. There were wobbly caravans of small donkeys, camels, and cows burdened with huge bundles of goods, and pint-sized burros straining under bales of sticks twice their size. Camels carried mounds of rugs and other hand-spun textiles. Bearded men in long, tattered robes and thin sandals shuffled by, sheaves of cowhides balanced delicately on their heads. Women in ankle-length, dirt-smudged dresses had huge water jugs lashed to their backs. Even small children, many with the scars of crosses gouged into their foreheads, dragged bulky water jugs on flimsy wooden wagons. The children we saw had bloated stomachs and wore rags for clothes. Worst of all, the flies swarmed upon the smallest children, who stood crying as buzzing clumps affixed themselves to their noses, eyes, and mouths. Throughout Africa, these flies lay eggs in the children's eyes, producing the red, festering eye slits that too often presage childhood blindness. Doctors have told me that a quick round of antibiotics and a dose or two of antiseptic eye cream would cure most of these afflictions.

We entered the city square. Aksum's huge stone obelisks could be seen through the trees, like an African Stonehenge perched on a hillside. Quarried from single pieces of granite, these towering one thousand-year-old columns (like small Washington Monuments) were royal burial stones or victory markers commemorating great military conquests. The largest piece of cut stone in the world—weighing over 500 tons—lies fallen on its side. No one can really say how these gigantic obelisks were transported or erected, but the monks claim that it was done by the power of the Ark.

Surveying this struggling population of hard-pressed humanity on its dusty patch of dirt, it was hard to imagine that Aksum was at the center of one of the mightiest ancient nations. The city was once the capital of a kingdom that dominated the crossroads of Africa and Asia for a millennium. The first reports of this highly developed civilization are from AD 64, when the unknown writer of *The Periplus of the Erythraean Sea* described Aksum's ruler as "a prince superior to most and educated with a knowledge of Greek."[4] Centuries later, a Roman ambassador named Julian glowingly described Aksum as "the greatest city of all of Ethiopia."

Aksum's king wore linen garments embroidered with gold from his waist to his loins, and he rode a four-wheeled, elephant-drawn chariot shingled with gold plates. Merchants from Aksum traveled to India, Ceylon, and China. This culture adopted Christianity during the fourth century and now lays claim to the greatest archaeological prize of all time, the Ark of the Covenant.

THE WAY OF THE ARK

The Yeha Hotel sits high on a hill overlooking the city. Workers completed the hotel just a few weeks prior to our arrival, but it already looked fifty years old.

After Ecuba left, Joby and I took rooms, organized our gear, and ate lunch, a tasty variation of spaghetti and red sauce. The Italian occupation of Ethiopia during the 1930s introduced the country to Italian cooking. Today, even the most obscure restaurant in Aksum offers pasta. The Ethiopians say that when Mussolini invaded Ethiopia, he wanted to get the Ark and take it to Italy because he hungered for its power. The Ethiopians hid it from him, as they have done from others who have tried to take it. They claim that they have successfully protected the Ark of the Covenant for more than two thousand years. According to Ethiopians, a divine appointment from God gave them poverty so that they would only have the Ark to think about.

After lunch, Ecuba returned, leading an old man by the hand. "This is Birani Miscal," he said. "His name means 'Light of the Cross.' He is an elder from the church of the Ark, and I believe he will be able to answer your questions."

The old man appeared to be chiseled from an ancient block of black stone. I would soon learn that he was a respected leader in the village. He was well educated and could speak six languages.

"It is my pleasure to meet you," I said, extending a hand. Birani bowed and smiled, displaying yellow teeth behind his dark lips and gray, unruly beard.

Ecuba left us with Birani, who with a slow wave motioned for us to follow him down the hill, across a field, and into Aksum's expansive church compound. A tree-shaded, mud-walled courtyard surrounded the old stucco church that has been an Aksum landmark for three hundred years. Its heavy wood doors were stained and sandblasted by the elements. Birani gestured toward a moss-covered rock wall that keeps women out. Around the outside of the wall, nearly filling a field, hundreds of linen-wrapped women knelt in prayer, chanting hymns and uttering melodic devotions.

"What are these women doing?" I asked.

"They come here every day to pray," Birani replied. "They are not allowed to go inside the church. It is a holy site. Most of these women are here because they cannot conceive a child, so they pray to the Ark of the Covenant to give them a child. If a woman becomes pregnant after praying in front of the church, she gives her firstborn son to the hermitage as a gift." He pointed to a cluster of old buildings nearby. "There the boys live a life of devotion and spend their days reading Scripture and fasting." He paused and then added, "It is where they become initiated into the ways of the Ark."

TIE A YELLOW RIBBON

Joby and I followed Birani into the small church, where several bearded, white-turbaned men stood like statues, praying with their eyes closed.

"Take off your shoes," Birani said. "To wear shoes in the church is sacrilege." We did so.

The sour odor of unwashed bodies and pungent incense filled the dark, thick-walled chamber. A cloud of candle smoke hung near the high-beamed ceiling. Some priests and monks propped their chins on tall sticks.

"Praying sticks," Birani explained. "They keep the monks from falling down during long prayer times." He handed us two such staves from a wooden cupboard on the back wall.

No one looked up. They paid no attention to the Americans dressed in khaki shirts and pants. All had lapsed into a trancelike state of worship, reciting a singsong chant in Tigrinya. Its cadence reverberated soothingly through the space.

"*Aaaah-yum, bay-yum. . . .*" Their chant vibrated in my bones.

I propped my chin on the hand-carved prayer stick as I had seen the monks do and stood in silence. Hours passed. I stole a look at Joby, who seemed to have fallen asleep. His eyes were closed, and his whole body leaned against the stick.

Narrow beams of light filtered through high wood lattice and illuminated a dim gallery of weathered paintings. Some depicted Jesus, the apostles, and Mary; others featured angelic hosts and local saints. The chapel's thick walls and recessed niches were smooth. Centuries of smoke, incense, and human sweat had burnished every surface.

A short recess was introduced by an oddly familiar, if barely audible, sound. I strained to hear a tiny speaker release a fuzzy version of "Tie a Yellow Ribbon Round the Old Oak Tree." An inexpensive, plastic radio alarm clock signaled the end of prayer time. Joby opened his eyes and let a short, spontaneous chuckle escape. I gave him a sharp jab with my elbow. In these solemn quarters, the song was just a time marker, its incongruity overlooked by the monks.

Birani led us out into stark sunlight.

The time had come. "Birani, could you introduce me to the Guardian of the Ark?"

Birani slapped a hand over his mouth and shook his head. "No.

It is impossible to see the Guardian. I cannot do this." Without elaborating, he beckoned us to follow him across the church grounds.

One of the reasons I had come so far was to meet the Guardian of the Ark. Graham Hancock's book described him as a lone soul who had surrendered his entire life to protecting the Ark of the Covenant. He would die having already spoken the name of the next Guardian, one of the adult males who had grown up in the hermitage.

Since he was the only man alive allowed to see the Ark, I needed to talk to him. Apparently, that was not going to be easy.

CHURCHES AND CHAPELS

We walked to a deep, mossy trough, overgrown with grass and filled in with rubble. This trench, Birani told us, contained the ruins of the original Saint Mary of Zion Church, built by King Ezana in the fourth century AD. It had been a memorial to Ethiopia's dramatic conversion to Christianity. It was also, according to tradition, where the Ark had once rested. The newer Saint Mary of Zion was built in the 1960s by Emperor Haile Selassie as a final resting place for the Ark.

"It is the most sacred place in Ethiopia," he said in hushed tones. We stared into the pit filled with ancient foundation stones. These were the crumbling remains of the earliest Christian church on the African continent.

I turned my eyes to the small chapel silhouetted by the setting sun. Somewhere within its thick cinder-block walls sat what all Ethiopia believes to be the original Ark of the Covenant.

The older men around us sat under a wide shade tree, wrapped in heavy multicolored prayer shawls and blankets, with a pot of water by their side. Others leaned against medieval rock-and-mortar pillars, reading red-bound Bibles. The entire place was awash in ghostly shadows, the congregation lost in a trance of personal devotion, their noses buried in *Ge'ez* translations of the Scriptures. Beneath a gnarled, old tree sat a lone man with a Kalashnikov machine gun.

"It is time to go," Birani said, and he took us back to our hotel for the night.

THE ADMINISTRATOR

During the night, a chill crept through the open windows into my room. I wasn't sleeping well, and the cold woke me. Relentless dreams of a gold box spewing flames and lightning haunted my mind. An elusive holy object rested in a dark chamber a few hundred yards from where I lay. There was no use in trying to sleep.

It was early Sunday morning and still dark. Eager to get started, I dressed and went in search of a predawn breakfast. I stepped from the hotel into a tree-filled courtyard. A tiny woman sat on a wooden stool just outside the hotel restaurant. She was dressed in a stained cotton dress and wore a tattered shawl over her bowed head.

I watched as the woman spread freshly cut sprigs of grass on a tray that held several small finger cups. She poured a handful of green coffee beans from a small burlap sack onto a thick metal plate over hot coals. She fanned the glowing coals with a palm leaf, and the raw coffee beans began to roast. As she moved them about the steel surface with a bent coat hanger, the beans turned a dark chocolate brown. A trickle of smoke filled the cool morning air with their rich aroma.

As the woman lifted her head and smiled, I saw the tattooed black cross on her forehead. She showed me how to smell the roasting beans by cupping her hand and drawing the aromatic smoke to her face. I bent over, and the rich fragrance drifted up to me. She then slid the beans off the hot metal surface into a stone mortar, and using a section of iron rebar as a pestle, the woman began pounding the beans into fine granules. She added the ground beans to a traditional clay pot filled with boiled water and allowed the coffee to steep. A few minutes later, she poured a steaming cup of espresso and served it to me with a slab of toasted bread smeared with tart marmalade. For a few moments, these delicacies took my mind off the Ark.

Dawn's first light brought Birani shuffling up the winding road to the restaurant's stone terrace. I wondered how he knew I'd be there at such an early hour. Without pleasantries, he solemnly informed me that he had arranged a private meeting with the administrator of Saint Mary of Zion Church, the official next-highest to the Guardian of the Ark. Birani then left for church services, having declined my offer of bread and coffee. Later I learned that it was one of the 250 or more fasting days the Ethiopian clergy keep each year. He would eat nothing that day.

I left Joby sleeping and strolled down to Saint Mary's courtyard. Hundreds of white-robed worshippers swayed, chanting a ritual that has endured since Christianity came to Ethiopia. The sun ascended almost unnoticed, splashing off the church's ancient clay buttresses. The church's coarse, smoke-stained stonework and sun-baked cornices made a beautiful backdrop to the slow but colorful pageant of monks carrying multicolored umbrellas. Hundreds of shawl-swathed followers trailed after them.

Hours passed as I watched the worshipping masses. Their dedication moved me. I felt a hand on my shoulder and turned to see Birani's yellow eyes and aged mahogany face.

"The tribunal will meet you now," he said.

I thanked him and told him I needed to return to the hotel first. I sprinted up the hill to the hotel and banged on Joby's door. A groggy Joby answered.

I was winded, but I managed to snap, "Get dressed. They want to see us, and they want to see us now!"

Joby, who had apparently been luckier at sleeping than I had been, threw on his clothes while I changed into a fresh white shirt. We soon rejoined Birani, who led us to the tribunal of five white-robed priests who sat waiting for us. My stomach was doing cartwheels.

A man named Narud sat at the head of the table. Birani introduced him as the Administrator of the Ark. He was tall, slender, and pleasant. He had a thin gray beard, and his eyes sparkled. He wore a long ceremonial robe with a turban wrapped high on his head. Hanging from his neck was an ornate wooden crucifix. He held a pale-green lime which he fingered incessantly.

This was my golden opportunity, and in my enthusiasm, I almost blew it. My first question betrayed my poor sense of protocol. "May we please meet the Guardian of the Ark?"

Birani winced, and my cartwheeling stomach seized. The priests shook their heads and cast glances at one another. I knew I had blundered.

Narud stroked his beard. I sensed my affront but had as yet acquired no feel for the culture. Birani, embarrassed, began to translate, but he needn't have bothered.

"Many have come before you, asking the same question," Narud said. His tone was stern. "They have been turned away."

Acknowledging my error, I asked another awkward question. "Has anyone but the Guardian ever seen the Ark?"

Narud grinned like a patient father but didn't answer right away. The others shifted in their chairs. Seconds ticked by, and finally Narud spoke in his heavily accented English. Still, he motioned for Birani to translate.

"No one but the Guardian has seen the Ark in this generation. This is as it should be. Neither will the world see it or photograph it or touch it—ever. It is forbidden." His gentle face turned severe, and his tone turned hard as steel. "We are entrusted with guarding the Ark of the Covenant." He placed the lime on the table. "It is our sacred commission to conceal its powers and protect its holiness."

The other priests sat in silent deference to Narud. I came to understand that this judiciary was the official buffer and first line of defense for the Ark's Guardian. In the single minute it had taken Narud to answer my first two questions, I had also seen that they possessed an unshakable belief that the sacred relic—the authentic Ark of the Covenant constructed at the foot of Mount Sinai to carry the Ten Commandments—now resided in their humble monastery.

Narud explained that in addition to this priestly order, the entire population—including members of the church and the Christian peoples of Tigray—considered it their birthright to protect the holy Ark. If foolhardy treasure hunters or a foreign invasion stormed Aksum and tried to steal the Ark, the intruders would experience the savage side of these gentle villagers. Each would gladly die in its defense, wielding machetes and machine guns cached from their many years of civil war. They would lay down their lives rather than compromise their sacred duty.

I changed the subject. "Does the Ark still have its powers?"

Narud leaned back. "Yes."

Turning to Birani, I asked, "Does this mean that the Ark still manifests the powers described in the Bible?"

The question made everyone uneasy. Only the day before, Birani had alluded to the Ark's powers, describing how barren women were able to conceive under its divine influence. Still, I had something more in mind. I knew of unconfirmed reports that the Ark manifested powers similar to those described in the book of Exodus. Some suggested that former rulers of Ethiopia had not only believed in the Ark's undiminished powers but also had, as in the days of Joshua, employed the relic in battle. In certain cases, according to legend, it provided a source of spiritual strength and raw power against aggressors.

Why would the Ark have any power today? I wondered. Hadn't the thick curtain that hid the Ark by separating the Holy of Holies from the rest of the Temple been torn from top to bottom? Didn't Christ on the cross end the old covenant by saying, "It is finished"? Wouldn't that have emptied the Ark of its power, leaving only a dormant golden husk? I doubted that any of these tales had even a smattering of truth. The Ark's supposed power (if the Ark still existed) was nothing but hyperbole, sensationalized by a culture immersed in its worship, a myth fortified by each retelling. Yet the Ethiopians insisted that the Ark still had mysterious, lingering powers.

Before we left, I asked Narud to describe the Ark. He held up his hand and said, "As it has been for the last thousand years, so it will be for the next thousand. As it is described in the Bible, so it is today."

His tone told me that our interview had ended.

Joby and I thanked the priests. With many smiles and hand-shakes, we pulled out a bag of medicine—antibiotics, aspirin, anti-septic creams, adhesive bandages—that I had packed as a goodwill offering. Then I handed Birani one hundred Ethiopian birr and asked him to tell the priests that they should use it to buy tea.

They seemed grateful but maintained their hard countenance toward us. I hadn't often experienced such steely indifference, even in closed Muslim cultures where everyone, it seemed, had their price and where most roadblocks could be negotiated with a bit of charm and ingenuity. These monks did not express even the slight-est interest in money or gifts. They are so devout that they wouldn't take an aspirin for a headache if they were fasting.

When I asked how they expected the world to believe that they had the Ark, they responded with looks of supreme indifference. They really don't care if anyone believes them or not. They live with a calm assurance that God has given them the task of protecting the Ark. They have no use for publicity and concern over what oth-ers think. They had no intention of divulging their secrets to me or to anyone else. I knew that my questions had become tiresome to them. It was time to go.

TEMPLE TRUMPETS

Joby and I thanked the priests again and followed Birani across the courtyard to the high iron fence at the rear of the chapel. As we waited, I inspected its well-fortified ramparts. The rear courtyard stood like a military bunker with its reinforced cinderblock walls framing a large walkout basement.

"There is where the Temple treasures are kept," Birani said.

After we had stood for fifteen minutes swatting flies in the hot sun, a smartly bearded temple guard, wearing a bright yellow robe, a white turban, and funky Ray-Ban sunglasses (no doubt a gift from a tourist), emerged from the dark basement. He strode to the fence and unlocked a long yellow box. Inside were the ornate crowns of several past kings. Sensing our indifference to the crown display, Birani exchanged some words with the man, who turned and went back in the building.

After several minutes the treasurer returned, carrying two long instruments bound tightly in linen. I thought at first that they might be ancient muskets, perhaps used in one of Tigray's civil wars. Then I noted their aged and tarnished appearance. I looked closer and realized they were hammered silver trumpets. The treasurer held them out briefly for our inspection, then laid them alongside the crowns.

Birani interpreted as the treasurer explained, "These trumpets have great value to Ethiopian orthodoxy. They are the original ceremonial trumpets from the First Temple in Jerusalem."

That stunned me. "Our tradition confirms it. Our ancestors recorded that the trumpets arrived in Ethiopia, along with the other Temple vessels, from Jerusalem."

I couldn't take my eyes off the heavily oxidized instruments. They were nearly five feet long and were covered with decorative engravings. They were forged of hammered silver, but they had a smoky bronzed appearance. If they were from the days of Solomon, they were nearly three thousand years old.

They looked vaguely familiar, and I tried to recall where I had seen such items before. Finally, I realized that these battered, pitted trumpets matched a pair that were carved into the Arch of Titus in Rome. That arch commemorates Titus's destruction of Jerusalem in AD 70, described by the Jewish historian Josephus as so thorough that even the walls and foundations of the street were decimated. "It was so thoroughly laid even with the ground by those that dug it up to the foundation that there was left nothing to make those that came thither believe it had ever been inhabited."[5]

Titus removed sacred vessels and treasures from the Second Temple, then paraded them through the streets of Rome in a victory celebration. These included the menorah, showbread table, and these silver trumpets, memorialized in 2 Chronicles 13:12: "So you see, God is with us. He is our leader. His priests blow their trumpets and lead us into battle against you. O people of Israel, do not fight against the Lord, the God of your ancestors, for you will not succeed!" (NLT).

Although Titus had despoiled the Second Temple, it made sense that the trumpets and vessels he took would be exact copies of those from Solomon's Temple. That meant that the long-necked trumpets carved into the Arch of Titus in Rome would match the appearance and dimensions of the First Temple trumpets made in the days of Moses. Scriptures indicate that God said to Moses, "Make two trumpets of hammered silver to be used for calling the community to assemble and for signaling the breaking of camp" (Numbers 10:1-2, NLT).

I could hardly believe it. Not four feet from me were what appeared to be the trumpets described in the Bible. Could these tarnished instruments be the ones forged in Old Testament days and placed by Solomon in the First Temple? When I pressed the keeper of the treasures for more details, he refused to elaborate. As with so many "facts" of Ethiopian heritage, the truth of the matter remained clouded.

On my first trip to this unusual corner of the world, I stumbled upon ancient treasures that seemed like bread crumbs along a fog-covered trail. I had already accepted that I would not be permitted to meet the Guardian of the Ark. Still, I wanted to visit a last sacred landmark, T'ana Kirkos Island on the mysterious Lake T'ana, some two hundred miles to the south. According to tradition, this holy island was the first hiding place of the Ark of the Covenant in Ethiopia for more than eight hundred years. When talking to Graham Hancock, the monks living on the island had mentioned an ancient altar high on a cliff where blood sacrifices had been performed by the ancient Hebrews. This was where the Ark had rested for centuries, and I hoped to see that place.

Other tourists that we met in Aksum said they had tried in vain to see T'ana Kirkos. They had begged their travel agents, pleaded with local government officials, and even petitioned the Ethiopian Ministry of Tourism, but to no avail. Something about it remained off-limits to foreigners. These reports didn't sit well with us.

Ecuba had rejoined us outside the gate, having arranged for us to visit other historic sites in the area. "Ecuba," I said with tempered excitement, "I want to go to T'ana Kirkos Island. Can you make that happen?"

Ecuba stared at me. He paused, then bowed politely. "I will see what can be done." With that, he headed back to the Yeha Hotel, and there was nothing for us to do but wait.

MISGANA

By the time I returned to the hotel, Ecuba had already hung up the phone at the front desk. He said, "You can fly to Bahar Dar today, and Misgana will meet you. He will get you permission to go to T'ana Kirkos."

It sounded too good to be true. Ecuba explained that his enterprising friend Misgana worked for a Bahar Dar travel company called Jacaranda Tours. He had the connections that would get us on the island of the Ark.

Bolstered by Ecuba's encouraging news, Joby and I packed our bags and said good-bye to Birani. I had grown fond of the old monk, who in a short time had ushered us into the secretive realm of Aksum's priestly order of the Ark.

Ecuba sped us out of Aksum to the airport, where we bought tickets for the one-hour flight to Bahar Dar. After a short wait, the twin-engine Fokker 50 prop plane dropped out of the sky, rumbled to a stop among the grazing cattle, and opened its doors. We grabbed our bags and walked through the choking dust, flies, and bees to climb aboard. We braced ourselves as the plane bounced down the rocky runway, lifted off over the nearby cliffs, and banked over the Tekeze River.

The terrain below transitioned from arid high desert to a dark green countryside. As we approached Bahar Dar, I could see the majestic Blue Nile meandering on its way through the Sudan to Egypt's Nile Delta, where it would pour into the Mediterranean Sea. The river is fed by the enormous Lake T'ana—a body of water 6,000 feet above sea level that covers 3,673 square miles. Both the Blue and the White Niles engorge during Ethiopia's long rainy season, flooding the Blue Nile northward into Egypt. This surge from Lake T'ana and its network of rivers carries much of the loam responsible for the Nile Delta's remarkable fertility. Gazing down at the many rivers cutting through the landscape, my mind stuck on a verse I had read in the Bible: "My scattered people who live beyond the rivers of Ethiopia will come to present their offerings" (Zephaniah 3:10, NLT).

We landed at the Bahar Dar airport on a paved runway and stepped from the plane into an almost suffocating curtain of humidity. The air reeked of burning rubbish. We retrieved our bags in the terminal and found ourselves face-to-face with a handsome, lanky young man in his early twenties.

"Hello, Mr. Bob. I am Misgana." He had a pleasant face and a comfortable smile. "It is a pleasure to meet you. I have made arrangements for your trip to Lake T'ana. Please come with me."

I would soon learn that Misgana had a sharp mind and a keen wit. His winsome smile would charm everyone we met, including the ladies. The son of a peasant coffee merchant, he was now an up-and-coming entrepreneur in a poor land strangled by years of civil war.

Misgana led us to a waiting cab, and we were off to our hotel. At the city's edge, he called our attention to an old fire truck by the side of the road among jacaranda and flame trees. "Mr. Bob, that is our new fire truck. The prior one was destroyed by the fire chief, who took it for its first drive."

"First drive?" I was puzzled.

"Yes," Misgana answered. "The town got a shiny new fire truck, and we had it for only one day. The fire chief raced it down the street and crashed it; we now have our old one back." He threw his head back and laughed. "Welcome to Bahar Dar."

En route, Misgana filled us in. His good friend Gebeyehu Wogawehu, who worked for the Tourism and Information Department in Bahar Dar, had granted us very rare permission to visit T'ana Kirkos Island.

"You're kidding," I said.

"No," Misgana replied, "but there is one condition. Gebeyehu must accompany us and oversee our journey."

"No problem," I answered, unconcerned about who joined us so long as we could visit the island.

"These days," Misgana explained, "we seldom get requests from foreigners to visit Lake T'ana's holy island. It is why a government agent must travel along to make sure that visitors violate no customs or steal artifacts. The island contains many treasures."

I nodded. "I imagine it does."

Misgana added, "You will also have to pay Gebeyehu's salary, because he will have to take two days off work."

"It sounds fair to me," I agreed. *Two days' salary is a fair enough price for going to an island forbidden to tourists,* I thought.

HOLY LAKE T'ANA

Our government-appointed guide, Gebeyehu Wogawehu, met us at the pier at 5:30 AM. We had rented a lightweight, aluminum-hulled skiff for four people, and we departed into the dense darkness. It would take three-and-a-half hours of riding Lake T'ana's moss-green waves to reach the rocky shore of T'ana Kirkos Island.

Gebeyehu sat in the back of the boat, grinning. He had short hair and a round, smiling face. He refused to shed his bulky green jacket, even later in the day under a hot sun. Joby threw his pack down and parked himself along the railing near the bow, alternately napping and staring into the mist. I sat on a wooden bench at the stern, invigorated by the crisp morning coolness. A mile or two from shore, we passed a ragged flotilla of reed boats from which fisherman were tossing their nets.

The sight of the reed boats brought to mind a passage from the Bible: "Woe to the land shadowed with buzzing wings, which is beyond the rivers of Ethiopia, which sends ambassadors by sea, even in vessels of reed on the waters" (Isaiah 18:1-2).

The sun rose. The sky filled with squawking seagulls, and Egyptian geese skimmed the water for insects. Less than an hour into the journey, I lost sight of the shore. There was little to see except the rays of dawn glimmering on the water.

I had heard that as many as forty-five inhabited islands lay scattered across the lake. This mighty body of water, surrounded by dense mountain jungle, would be an obstacle to anyone looking for a lost Ark. Even with motorized boats and modern navigational charts, I felt as if we were traveling an uncharted ocean. Only the T'ana natives and a handful of guides know where most of the islands lay. Without an expert guide and some knowledge of T'ana's monastic cultures, the Ark's resting place would remain a secret.

"Do you know much about this lake, Misgana?" I asked.

"I grew up on one of the islands," he answered. "I know this lake well. When I was a boy, my father would take me on his little boat. He traveled to the islands to sell coffee beans."

"Did he sell coffee beans on T'ana Kirkos?"

Misgana shook his head. "No, Mr. Bob. We never went to T'ana Kirkos. No one goes there."

His words made me realize how fortunate I was. Misgana was a local, but this would be his first time to the island. What kind of island was so secret that even the locals didn't visit?

I was determined to find out.

Misgana raised his hand and extended one of his narrow fingers. "There, Mr. Bob. There is T'ana Kirkos."

THE LOST ISLAND

From a distance, the island revealed little more than leafy trees and breaking surf, but the closer we came, the more impressive it grew. Tall cliffs hunkered near the shore, their thick foliage crowned by primeval trees and towering cacti. Nearer still, I could make out a small hut on one of the cliffs. Overhead, three kingfishers circled, scouting for Nile perch.

The captain steered the boat into a shady lagoon. As he pulled close to the orange rocks, I saw a thin flight of granite steps chiseled into the cliff. After tying off, Misgana ushered Joby, Gebeyehu, and me onto the rocks and up the steps under the jungle canopy.

Joby and I left our camping gear on the boat. If the monks consented, we hoped to spend the night, though both Misgana and Gebeyehu cautioned us that no outsider, so far as they knew, had ever slept overnight on the island.

"I do not think the monks will allow it," Gebeyehu declared.

Still, if the opportunity presented itself, I wanted to be ready. We could use the extra time to poke around and see what curiosities might be present.

I knew that Graham Hancock never got to tour the island in detail. He interviewed the chief priest, asked a few questions, and hiked up to the altar, but he was shown very little. I felt that certain clues and evidence remained hidden, and I was prepared to spend as much time with them as they would allow.

Within minutes of our arrival, my optimism crumbled. Hiking down the narrow trail to meet us, T'ana Kirkos's chief priest, in his loose, flowing white robe and turban, stopped us in our path. He strode up to Misgana and Gebeyehu and immediately began peppering them with questions. His filthy prayer shawl was thrown backward over his shoulders. He seemed none too pleased to see us.

After a few moments of heated discourse, Misgana backed away and whispered, "The village elder will not let you on the island if you are not an Orthodox Christian."

"What?"

Misgana shrugged. "He wants to know if you are Orthodox. He will not allow us to go any farther unless we are professed Orthodox Christians."

Not certain what he meant by "Orthodox Christian," I was unsure how to respond, but I hadn't come this far to be turned away in the first minutes of my arrival. I stepped to the priest and asked Misgana to translate.

"I am Bob Cornuke of the United States, and I am a Christian. I would like to come onto your island and learn more about your culture."

Misgana relayed my message to the dispassionate monk, who answered in Amharic, staring straight into my eyes.

"He wants to know if you are an *Orthodox* Christian," Misgana repeated.

I sensed this was the moment when everything could implode. "Ask him this: When he says his prayers does he pray in the name of the Orthodox Christian Church or to Jesus?"

Misgana translated and gave me a reply. "He says, 'To Jesus.'"

"Then tell him that we pray to the same God." I pointed to the priest. "We are Christian brothers; we are followers of Jesus."

I held out my hand. The priest hesitated and then smiled wryly as if conceding the mental chess match. After a moment, Misgana turned and said, "Abba says you are welcome."

The priest named Abba (meaning "father") bowed slightly and approached me with an outstretched hand, shaking mine with his right hand while holding my wrist with his left—a gesture of honor and respect. A lengthy greeting ensued, after which the priest led us up the overgrown path through a stone archway and into a grassy clearing. There we saw a couple of dilapidated shacks and a few raggedly dressed monks. The holy men were stunned to see us.

After a brief round of introductions, they led us higher up the path toward their village, which sat on a hillside, choked with scrub and alive with hummingbirds and starlings. We walked under a canopy of vines. Along the path, I looked up and received a sudden shock. Concealed in the thick, green mantle hung a curtain of spiderwebs crawling with dozens of fat-bellied, long-legged spiders, some larger than my fully outstretched hand.

"Are they poisonous?" I asked Misgana.

"Yes, they are poisonous," Misgana replied, "but they are not aggressive. I have seen the monks let them crawl up their arms. They rarely bite."

I wasn't going to test the truth of that statement. I ducked under the webs, glancing up to see spiders scrambling in all directions. When we reached the village, the compound struck me as depressingly glum. It was little more than a small circle of dirty thatched huts. There were no creature comforts.

"Where are the monks?" I asked.

"Most of the monks are still at work on the other side of the island," Misgana explained. "They tend the monastery's fields of teff, coffee, and vegetables."

I peered west and saw a marshy finger of land stretching away from the main island, connected to another half-submerged sliver of peninsula. From a distance, I could just make out the bobbing white robes of monks toiling in the heat.

On the ground about us lay dusty piles of unshucked coffee berries. A few young boys gathered about us. They were dressed in tattered prayer shawls that looked as if they had never been washed. The boys stared at us.

I didn't immediately ask about the Ark, preferring instead to spend that first afternoon and evening watching their routine. Over the course of those hours, I gained a feel for the rhythms of the village and sensed that the chief priest was warming to me.

Shortly before the evening meal, we met the rest of the order as the sweaty, dirty band of monks straggled into camp. One of them walked with the aid of a staff. Even at a distance I could see that his foot was injured. A deep, angry-looking wound oozed from his instep. They told me that he had injured himself while swinging an ax. The blade had missed the log and found his foot. He had been living with this wound for several weeks. I could see gray bone.

"Such injuries are common on the islands," Misgana explained.

I believed him, since I could see a variety of discolored, swollen, deeply scarred limbs. The poor fellow's foot had swollen to twice its normal size. With no medicine or antiseptic to fight the infection, the prognosis wasn't good.

I couldn't sit by and do nothing. "Ask Abba if he would allow us to help the monk."

Misgana did so. "He says it is permitted."

Joby and I took the monk aside, cleansed and bandaged the wound, then gave him a heavy dose of antibiotics. We also handed him a month's supply of capsules, enough—we hoped—to help.

The monks asked us to join them in their evening meal, and we followed them to a smoke-filled grass hut. It took several seconds to adjust to the darkness inside, but soon I could make out an old man stooped over a black pot. It was resting on a pile of coals, and he was stirring the contents with a flat, broken stick. The lumpy brown concoction in the pot smelled horrible.

The man looked up and gave a toothless smile, then dug out a paddle full of the stuff and slopped it in one of the wooden bowls stacked beside him. I bowed and took the steaming bowl of whatever-it-was and stood waiting for the group of monks to join us. One by one the monks filed in, got their bowl, and left.

"Where are they going?" I asked Misgana.

"To eat," he said.

Unsure if I should follow, I walked behind the group of monks. They scattered about the village and entered small huts. These huts were little more than thatched boxes, no larger than a file cabinet tipped on its side. They were made of tightly woven palm branches that harbored nests of leggy spiders and other insects. There were no windows. They were the most austere living quarters I had ever seen.

When asked to join the group in their evening meal, I had assumed that it would be a communal gathering. I was wrong. Here you got your food and left to eat it alone. I couldn't imagine living in those bleak, woven-palm cubicles, but that's all they had in the world. They slept, prayed, ate their meals, and endured their monastic lives here from childhood to death. The island was their home, their universe.

After the meal (I had covertly dumped my whatever-it-was and eaten a granola bar in private), the monks brought out another suffering soul. He was an old man sprawled on a mat of palm fronds and groaning with every movement. He had contracted a severe infection in his groin. The pain had become so intense that for days he had been unable to walk. I snatched a pair of rubber gloves and some topical antibiotic cream from my pack.

I handed the items to Joby and said, "Put some of this on the infection."

Joby shot me a look as if I'd skinned his favorite hunting dog. "What?" he whispered, glancing down at the pus-filled ulceration.

"Here," I insisted.

With a long sigh, Joby pulled on the rubber gloves and began smearing on the cream; he acted as if he were handling rusty razor blades, as he carefully daubed away. We left the man still wincing, yet thanking us with great sincerity.

"You owe me, Bubba! You owe me big!" Joby repeated as we left the monks' village.

WHAT HAVE WE DONE?

As I had hoped, Abba decided to let us spend the night on the island. Joby and I could set up our tents on the cliff above the village. Misgana said that the privilege should be regarded as a rare honor.

As it had been for the last one thousand years, the monks turned in at dusk. They would rise, as always, by 4:00 AM for prayers. Joby

and I gathered our gear and hiked to the highest point of the island, pitching camp on a spine of ridge barely wide enough to support our tent. In these compact quarters, merely rolling over in our
sleep might send us hurtling off the cliff onto the rocks of the lagoon, so we cleared the area of leaves and placed a ring of large
stones around our tent to stop us if we should begin to slide.

A fresh breeze blew in off the lake, and a bank of thin clouds
draped the moon. The dark skies dazzled with stars, and Lake
T'ana—black, sullen, and immense—seemed to mingle with the
heavenly expanse. Then I noticed the buzzing. By making a tent
site and brushing away the leaves on this ancient cliff, we had
stirred up thousands of creeping and winged insects from their
nests. Then the mosquitoes came on. To counter the attack, Joby
and I slathered ourselves with an entire bottle of mosquito repellent, knowing that malaria was rampant on these islands. I started
a fire and stoked it with rotting tree branches. The billowing
smoke cloud and the repellent kept the insects at bay.

At last we could sit down and relax. I nudged the fire with a stick,
prodding the embers to release a little more heat. Through the gray
smoke, I could see a row of white eyes staring at us from the dense
palm leaves behind Joby. Curious monks, no doubt, had come up
to spy on the crazy Americans.

I waved them in, and after several moments, one of the bolder
ones tiptoed to the edge of our makeshift camp. He was a boy no
more than fourteen years old, probably an apprentice from a
nearby island. I stood up, and he jumped back into the security of
the green foliage, startled by my sudden movement.

"Joby, hand me a candy bar," I whispered.

Joby rummaged in his pack and pulled out a chocolate bar. I

handed it to the boy, motioning for him to take a bite. The monk chomped down on the Snickers, wrapper and all. Not only had these island dwellers never seen a candy bar, but they had no idea what to make of a wrapper. In slow motion, I walked over and unwrapped the candy. The young man took a nibble, then a bite. After he swallowed, a smile crossed his face. Suddenly six other boys— all between fourteen and eighteen years of age—leaped out from the darkness. All wanted Snickers bars.

The older monks had gone to bed; the night belonged to the young. After endless nights of prayer, eating alone, and candles out by 7:30, they acted as if the circus had come to town. Joby and I handed out more candy and watched, amused, as the boys gobbled it up. After a strict diet of vegetables and sour *injera*, the spongy flatbread that is a part of every Ethiopian meal, that first bite of chocolate must have exploded sweetly in their mouths. Unfortunately, their pure young bodies were unaccustomed to sugar and chocolate; they soon began bounding about the ridge like ferrets on a double latte.

Joby took out our two-way radios and turned them on. After a short demonstration, two boys started shouting at each other through the radios, scurrying about the ridge. I took out my night-vision binoculars and showed them how to see in the dark. Seconds later they had commandeered the binoculars and taken them over to the cliff, where they peered down into the village. They began giggling uncontrollably. I walked over to see that they had undertaken a bit of island espionage, watching the older monks coming and going from the village outhouse, which was a woven palm mat with a hole in it situated at the edge of the lake. Soon the boys began laughing out loud. They fought each other for the binoculars and viewed with hilarity proceedings that had, until that very moment, been private.

"Joby," I said, "what have we done?"

The boys were now running amok. Prior to our arrival, T'ana Kirkos had experienced twenty-five hundred years of uninterrupted solitude. Now, laughing boys buzzing from sugar and bewitched by fancy gadgets ran through the jungle as if drunk on moonshine. In one brief interchange, I feared, we had unraveled centuries of religious tradition. I turned to Joby, who was watching the youthful antics with a mixture of delight and concern.

"Joby," I whispered, ducking sparks as one boy tripped over the fire pit while jabbering into a radio, "it took them twenty-five hundred years to build this unique island culture of repose and solitude—and we've wrecked it in just twenty minutes."

TEMPLE VESSELS

Bong! Bong! Bong!

Prying my eyes open, I squinted at my watch. It was just after 4:00 AM, under a black sky. A few Yemen fireflies circled in front of the tent flap. I crawled from our tent, shuffled over to the cliff, and looked down to see a young monk clobbering a spent .50-caliber artillery shell with a fat stick. Someone had hung the rusty Russian casing by a string to use as a dinner/wake-up bell. Aside from a sooty cooking pot down by the village, it was the first refined metal I had seen on the island. A soldier, who had perhaps grown up on one of these islands, had dropped it off from the mainland.

I shook Joby awake. The night before, we had been invited to attend the monks' morning prayer service, and we needed to move quickly if we were to make it on time. I inspected our camp and saw a few wadded up candy wrappers stuck in some bushes, the only evidence of the previous night's chaos. Our two-way radios, slightly worse for wear, lay intact on opposite sides of the camp; the night-vision binoculars, smudged with soot, had been abandoned next to the campfire pit.

The evening's riotous events had come to a swift halt not twenty minutes after they began when an elder monk appeared on the ridge. Framed in moonlight, he regarded with astonishment a scene he probably could never have conceived. He barked an order in Amharic, and suddenly the young monks scrambled off the ridge into the village and shut themselves in their Spartan sleeping hutches. In seconds, the island was silent. Joby and I both groaned, relieved that no disaster had occurred as a result of our meddling. I prayed that we had violated no sacred customs.

The morning echoed with the soothing jungle sounds of island birds and brisk lake breezes rustling the trees. The wind drifting off the vast lake reminded me of the Rocky Mountains after a morning rain, and I fought off a pang of homesickness.

Although I hadn't slept soundly, I felt energized and excited about what the day might bring. Joby and I pulled on our boots, damp with dew and teeming with bugs, and then padded our way down to the village. The monks had already begun to file into a small mud hut. Misgana strolled into camp, sleepy-eyed from his night on the boat. I told him what had happened on the ridge, and he just laughed.

Gebeyehu Wogawehu stood nearby in his green jacket, smiling. "Did you enjoy your campout, gentlemen?" I nodded, thinking that for a government-appointed chaperone, Gebeyehu had been all but invisible.

One of the boys from the previous evening stood smartly at the door, grinning shyly as he ushered us into the room. Inside, the unventilated hut reeked of centuries of sweating monks, dirty feet, moldering candle wax, and musky incense. A conical depression in the middle of the floor, at least a foot deep, spoke of untold generations of monks shuffling their feet during morning prayers.

We took our place in the back, and a young lad with a shaved head handed us prayer sticks. Considering these sessions can last a long time, I appreciated the prop.

Joby and I tried to join in, but within minutes, my calves and shins had begun to itch, then sting. I reached down to scratch and realized that the hut was infested with fleas—not typical American fleas, but the feral African strain. My legs must have tasted like aged tenderloin compared to the monks' psoriasis-scarred limbs.

For the next three hours, the carnivorous fleas feasted inside my pant legs until I wanted to sprint from the hut, duck behind a tree, and strip down to my Skivvies. But I didn't. After our rough introduction and the young monks' revelry the night before, I didn't dare risk offending Abba by snubbing his prayer meeting. I had no feel for the island protocol, so I suffered in silence, praying for relief and for the vigil to end. Misgana told me later that I could have left at any moment without the slightest offense, but I imagined my quiet torment as a sort of penance that might earn me access to the island's secrets.

Three hours later, as the sun began to rise over the lake, the monks finally broke for breakfast. I rushed into the sunlight and pulled up the cuff of my pants to see a sweaty and inflamed leg, sheathed in a crimson rash that would not subside until I returned to the States. Raking the inside of my calves with my fingernails, I turned to Abba and, as casually as I could, mentioned that I'd read Graham Hancock's book *The Sign and the Seal*. He nodded, unmoved, so I asked about the Hebrew stone altar on the island's cliffs. He nodded again, this time mumbling a few words to Misgana.

Misgana leaned near and said, "Abba says he would be happy to show you."

BLOOD OF THE ALTAR

Abba led us up a narrow path bordered by prickly, overgrown bushes. A series of rough stone steps emptied out onto a narrow plateau at the island's summit.

"This is where the ritual blood sacrifices took place centuries ago by the Jewish caretakers of the Ark," Abba said, with Misgana translating.

Near the ledge stood a lichen-covered block of granite with a six-inch-square hole carved in its top. Judging from the thick layer of encrusted moss on it, the stone must have been hundreds, possibly thousands of years old.

Abba walked over and demonstrated how the holes in the columns had been used to collect blood during the ritual sacrifice of a lamb. Holding up an imaginary basin to illustrate how the ancient priests scattered blood over the stones, Abba pretended to pour the remaining blood into the hollows in the pillars. In both size and shape, the columns resembled the stone *masseboth* set up on high places in the earliest phases of the Hebrew religion. These ritual altars had served for sacrificial offering ceremonies much as Abba described.[6]

Abba showed us how the high priest dipped his right forefinger into a basin containing the blood, then scattered it over the stones and tent in an up-and-down, whiplike motion. He made a tipping movement, as if pouring blood from the imaginary basin into the cup-shaped hollows of the pillars. The manner in which he reenacted the sacrament seemed to mimic purification rites prescribed in the Old Testament book of Leviticus, chapters 4 and 5.

The granite altar did indeed seem appropriate to the ancient Hebrew ritual. But where did the Ark fit in? Where did it sit beneath the Tabernacle? I knew the monks had never revealed to any outsider precisely where the Ark had sat on the island. The best they could offer Graham Hancock was that it lay "somewhere near" the cliffs where we now stood.[7]

With nothing to lose, I decided to ask, "Abba, where did the Ark sit?" My heart skipped a beat when he casually pointed to the smooth granite beneath my feet.

"The Ark sat right here?" I asked, looking down.

"Yes," he said, nodding.

He explained, and Misgana relayed the words in English. "He says the Ark sat here, on this ledge, so that the blood could also be sprinkled on the Tabernacle at the time of the sacrifice. This tradition has been passed down through the centuries." This confused me since the Bible makes no mention of sprinkling blood on the Tabernacle.

I stared at the smooth surface of rock, perched high above the lagoon and surrounded on all sides by sheer cliffs. As a formidable watchtower from which to repel invaders, the ledge made perfect sense as a place for the Ark. I bent down to inspect the granite surface, an unremarkable table of stone covered in decaying leaves and layers of thatch.

I turned to Joby. "If the Tabernacle sat here . . . ," I said, pausing, then thinking out loud. "If the Tabernacle sat here, balanced on a solid slab of rock, how could a tent be secured over it? The winds whipping up this high would blow any freestanding structure into the lagoon." I looked around. "Are there tent pegs or socket holes for tent poles to fit in? There must be. If we could find evidence of the Tabernacle on this plateau, it would lend weight to Abba's claim."

I got down on my knees and began poking around, pushing leaves and thatch aside and feeling for something—I wasn't sure what. I took out my knife and slid it down through the thick thatch, poking and prodding, sticking it into rocks and cracks, searching for a spot where the granite might yield to emptiness. Misgana, Joby, and Abba stared at me, clearly perplexed, but after a few minutes my knife found a hollow indentation in the rock.

"Here!" I said, quickly scooping out the dirt and leaves. "Joby, come help me."

Together we cleared the area. After some more digging, we managed to clean out a clearly defined socket hole, hidden beneath centuries of decayed organic matter, where workers could have anchored a tent pole. It sat approximately twenty-five feet from what Abba had called the altar of pillars, precisely where the Tabernacle of the Ark had once stood.

I began clearing the rest of the ledge, probing the leaves and debris with my knife. After some minor excavation, I found a second hole, roughly the same circumference as the first. Six inches of rotting palm fronds had been covering it. While not quite as pronounced as the first, this one sat closer to the ledge and appeared to have been eroded by time.

I scoured the rest of the slab but never found the other two tent holes. By the look of the ledge, the rock where the other holes would have been carved had been chipped and worn away by wind and erosion.

I noticed a small pile of rocks stacked next to the altar—a makeshift shrine? Among the chunks sat a sizable piece of granite with a tent-pole-sized hole carved in the top. By appearances it might have been a third socket hole, long since broken away from the ledge. Who knew? Abba didn't, and after a few more minutes of scraping in the leaves, I told Joby, "I think we've found all we're going to find up here."

As we walked back down the trail, my mind swirled with provocative scenarios. Had we just stood on the *Shetiyyah* of T'ana Kirkos, the foundation stone of an ancient Ethiopian Holy of Holies? Had I hollowed out the contours of the tent holes that had once supported the Tabernacle of the Ark? Were Joby and I the first Westerners to learn of the Ark's location on the cliffs? I noticed Abba eyeing me with some interest, his expression registering an uneasy tension at the discovery of the tent-peg holes, as if he had never seen them.

"I don't think they knew the holes were there," Misgana whispered.

It didn't surprise me. The ledge clearly hadn't been maintained, and the tent holes probably seemed a matter of minor consequence to the ancient monks after the Ark departed.

"Joby," I said, "if those holes signify what I think they do, then both of us stood precisely where the holy Ark once sat. We stood where the Tabernacle and the Holy of Holies would have been."

After two hours of exploring, we walked back to the village. We stopped as Abba pointed to a long, narrow fissure in a rock wall, which he said contained the skeleton of one of the original Hebrews who brought the Ark to the island more than two thousand years ago. They had buried the Hebrew in one of the island's huge, V-shaped cracks in the granite cliff and then covered it over with tons of stones.

THE GOMER

Back at the village, Abba led us to a thick-walled hut and unlocked heavy wooden doors. He disappeared inside the darkened room for a moment while Joby and I waited outside.

"I believe the elder has something else to show you," Misgana said.

Emerging a few minutes later, Abba placed a small mat on the ground for us to sit on. He laid another mat a few feet in front of us. Then he instructed someone to help him carry over a large basin. It was broad and shallow, approximately two feet wide and no more than a couple of inches deep. A green patina from many years of oxidation made it difficult for me to identify the metal. I guessed that it was bronze.

Abba explained, "The ancient Hebrews who brought the Ark to Lake T'ana called it a *gomer*. They used it up on the cliffs to collect the blood used in the ritual sacrifices. The priest would stir the blood in the basin to keep it from getting thick."

THE METAL STAND

Abba reentered the storage hut and returned, balancing a heavy, bulky tangle of metal in his hands. It was a single stand of what appeared to be iron rods fused to a ring at the top and bottom. Abba told us that it had once been a sturdy stand to hold the bronze bowl but had long since collapsed from metal fatigue and extreme age. Its edges were mottled and encrusted with the same bluish pits and corrosion as the bowl, but it had a deep, red-brown oxidation. The opening at the top of the stand seemed to be about the same dimensions as the bronze basin, so it made sense that this was the stand for it.

Cradling the basin like a newborn baby, Abba again described how his predecessors had used it to scatter blood in the ancient Hebrew fashion. The more I looked, the more the basin and stand seemed to reflect passages in Exodus and Leviticus describing the basin and stand as an integrated unit for ritual cleansing (Exodus 30:17-19). Or it could have held the sacred anointing oil used to consecrate the Tabernacle (Exodus 30:26). Both the basin and stand also appear in Leviticus, when Moses ordained Aaron and his sons for the priesthood (Leviticus 8:10-11). But Abba and his predecessors interpreted the basin as an instrument for blood sacrifice. It didn't really matter. These implements possibly shared a Hebrew origin, and the monks on T'ana Kirkos had neither the resources nor the technology to forge metal. Someone had obviously brought them here.

I thought of the silver trumpets at the Aksum chapel and wondered if this basin and stand had been among the original Temple vessels, forged in Moses' time and placed in Solomon's Temple for service before the Ark. Had these instruments actually come to T'ana Kirkos with the Ark?

The monks insisted that they had.

MEAT FORKS AND ALMOND BUDS

"Mr. Bob!" Misgana whispered, nudging me. Abba had just reemerged from the hut holding a two-pronged instrument that looked like two long, thin spears fastened together. I quickly identified it as consistent with yet another Hebrew sacrificial implement, a meat fork used to burn sacrifices over ritual fires.

"Abba says it is a meat fork," Misgana said, "left on the island by those who brought the Ark."

Heavily rusted and showing signs of wear similar to the basin and stand, the implement's long double prongs met at a horizontal bridge at the top, crowned by what I took to be an old Aksumite cross.

Abba corrected me. "It is not a cross but the image of a budding almond flower."

An almond flower? My mind drifted back to Saudi Arabia and the mountain called Jabal al-Lawz, which in English means "Mountain of the Almond Flower."

Throughout the Old Testament, the budding almond ranked high in Israel's sacred iconography, adorning many vessels used in the Tabernacle and in the First Temple (Exodus 25:33-36; 37:19-22). One of the great Bible stories is of Aaron's almond staff miraculously budding overnight (Numbers 17:8). That same staff, regarded as the sign of one of Yahweh's great Old Testament miracles, came to lie alongside the holy manna and the Ten Commandments within the Ark of the Covenant (Hebrews 9:4).

Meat forks, bronze basins, bronze stands—the pieces were fitting better than I could have hoped. As far as I knew, no Westerner had ever seen these items. Had they indeed once served in the Temple of Solomon? It seemed a far reach for the monks to make that claim, but then, there they were, sitting right in front of us. The monks insisted that their ancient writings and traditions marked these items as the genuine artifacts from the Bible.

If I had only seen one or two of these artifacts, I might have written it off as coincidence. Yet taken together—the cliff shrine, the pillars for blood sacrifice, the hidden tent holes, and now the basin, stand, and meat fork—we seemed to have uncovered interlocking pieces of a fantastic puzzle. Each of these vessels and components appeared much like those described in Scripture; each made an arguable case for T'ana Kirkos as an ancient Hebrew haven; and each suggested at least the possibility that this might have been a resting place for the Ark of the Covenant.

I turned to Abba. "Would you allow me to scrape off a bit of metal from the *gomer* or the meat forks to take back to my country to test?" I knew his answer before I asked, but I had to ask. Abba frowned and shook his head.

"No, Mr. Bob," Misgana said. "Under no circumstances can you do such a thing. These are sacred vessels."

After a time, I stood and took a deep breath. Overhead I saw an enormous, white-tailed eagle gliding over the cliffs. I thanked Abba for his kindness and for showing me more than I ever expected to see. My mind was darting from one fact to another as I tried to put all this in perspective. In a word, I was stunned.

The hours were passing quickly, and we still faced a long boat ride back to our departure point. Gebeyehu Wogawehu was waiting by the boat. He had offered us two days of his time, and that time was nearly gone.

"Joby, let's get our things together. It's time to go," I said with reluctance.

Sunlight had faded into dusk. It had been a full, profitable day, and our pilot didn't like to be out on the water much past dark. I could leave now, satisfied. We bid farewell to Abba and the other monks and donated a bag of medicine and some money. Hauling gear down the trail to the lagoon, we turned to see a small, frail-looking monk shuffling after us.

I didn't recognize him at first. "Joby, that's the man with the infection you treated with antibiotic cream."

Joby did a double take, then yelled, "He's walkin'."

The man beamed. And he walked straight, something I was told he hadn't been able to do for weeks. As he approached, he extended his hands, and in his calloused fingers we saw three shriveled limes.

"It is an offering of thanks," Misgana said. "It is all he has."

Realizing that this old monk wanted to give us what were probably his life's possessions, Joby and I reluctantly accepted the gift. We bowed toward one another, exchanging grateful smiles. Then, with tears in his eyes, the old monk began thanking us with extravagant smiles and gestures of gratitude. He slipped down to his knees and kissed my leg.

"He is in your debt and asks you to take the limes as a blessing," Misgana said. "He didn't think he'd ever walk again."

I carefully placed the limes in my bag and said good-bye. We loaded our gear onto the skiff and helped the pilot push off. I turned to see Abba walking down the trail. Suddenly he turned and stood on the rocks, smiling and waving good-bye.

"You have made new friends, Mr. Bob," Misgana offered, hopping down from the bow. He tossed his tiny pack into the cabin and then added, "Abba told me they would welcome you back anytime."

Of all the treasures that this journey yielded, those few words from a T'ana Kirkos holy man and the three limes in my bag made the trip for me. With the sun now lying low over Lake T'ana, we turned into the chop and headed south. The trip had been successful, and I was eager to return home. My first visit to Ethiopia had come and gone, but there would be many more.

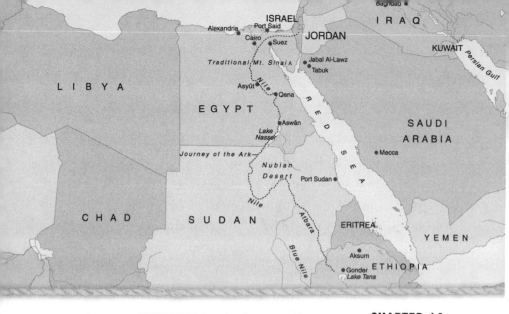

Colorado, 1998

In April 1998, I was home in Colorado, spending a lot of time por-
ing over sources in libraries. Unfortunately, I found few references
to the location of the Ark. One source suggested that King Shishak
of Egypt had looted the Temple and stolen treasures of gold and
silver. This theory was the basis for the movie *Raiders of the Lost Ark*.
Another popular theory is that King Nebuchadnezzar of Babylo-
nia destroyed the Ark when he invaded Israel in 598 BC. The apoc-
ryphal book of 2 Maccabees indicates that the Ark was hidden in a
cave on Mount Nebo, and there are recent claims by rabbis that
they have seen the Ark in a tunnel under the Temple Mount. Others say that the Ark is hidden in a crypt below the Vatican. None of
the legends can be verified and most have no biblical foundation.

The Ark, it seems, went missing from the Temple, and no one knows what happened to it. Was it destroyed or has it somehow survived to this day? If someone destroyed the Ark, then surely a biblical chronicler would have noted it. Yet Scripture doesn't even hint that such an event took place. The Ark simply ceased to be mentioned. To complicate matters, only one person—the Jewish high priest—would have known if the Ark was gone from the Temple. Once a year, on the Day of Atonement, the high priest entered the temple's Holy of Holies, carrying animal blood as a sacrifice for the sins of the people. It was his job to sprinkle the blood on the Ark and in front of the Ark. Because no one else went into the Holy of Holies, no one else would know if the Ark was gone. Its resting place is probably the best-kept secret in history.

Separating fact from fiction concerning the chain of events between Jerusalem and Ethiopia would take time, effort, and money. But there was really no other option if I wanted to find the answers. Jim Irwin used to say, "Be persistent and press on." I thought it was good advice, so I shouldered my pack and headed out.

I was on the road again.

ISRAEL FIRST

The Temple Mount was the last known biblically verified location of the Ark, so it seemed logical for me to start there and follow the trail to Ethiopia. In Jerusalem, I visited the Western Wall, also called the Wailing Wall. Jews come here to lament the old Temple's destruction and to pray that a new one will stand in its place. Many regard the Western Wall as a holy place. People write prayers on scraps of paper and tuck them into the cracks between the ancient stone blocks. Most believe that these blocks were the foundation stones of Solomon's Temple.

There I met several Jewish men from the Gondor region on Lake T'ana in Ethiopia. In 1984 the Israeli government airlifted them to Jerusalem with ten thousand other Falashas during a mission called "Operation Moses." They told me what I had heard in Ethiopia, that "the Ark of the Covenant is in a church in Aksum."

The Falasha religious leaders confirmed that for two hundred years, the Ark was in Egypt before continuing south to T'ana Kirkos Island. After another eight hundred years, the Ark was moved from T'ana Kirkos to Aksum by the Ethiopian king Ezana, and it remains there to this day. The Ethiopian Jewish community now living in Israel duplicated the comments of the Christian monks living on T'ana Kirkos Island.

I visited the Jerusalem Hebrew Institute, where I interviewed social anthropologist Dr. Shalva Weil to see if a historical record exists of Ethiopian Jews possessing the Ark. Dr. Weil described the Ethiopian Falasha Jews as modern descendants of Old Testament Hebrews who traveled to Egypt centuries ago. After settling in Egypt for a time, she said, they made their way south through Nubia (southern Egypt and northern Sudan) and eventually occupied northern Ethiopia. When I asked about the possibility that the Ark of the Covenant was taken by these Jews and was now resting at the chapel at Aksum, she smiled, drew a deep breath, and said, "There is a very strong conviction that the Ethiopian Christians possess the Ark."

The legendary evidence put the Ark in Egypt after it was taken from the Temple, but I wondered what biblical clues I might find to back up this supposition. There were plenty. As I gathered hints from Scripture and from Graham Hancock's research, I soon began to construct my own theory as to when the Ark left the Temple, why it had gone, and even where it had been taken.

The last known reference to the Ark's presence in the Temple was during Hezekiah's reign. The Bible doesn't explicitly say that the Ark was in the Temple, but this can be logically concluded because Hezekiah went up to the Temple and prayed this prayer before the Lord: "O Lord, God of Israel, you are enthroned between the mighty cherubim! You alone are God of all the kingdoms of the earth. You alone created the heavens and the earth" (2 Kings 19:15, NLT).

Because the Bible declares that the Lord dwells between the cherubim, and Hezekiah was praying to the Lord, whose manifested presence appeared above the Ark, it can be deduced that the Ark was then residing in the Temple (around 701 BC). However, the Ark was missing from the Temple prior to Josiah's reign (three kings after Hezekiah). We know this because Josiah spoke to his priests and said, "Put the holy ark in the house which Solomon the son of David, king of Israel, built. It shall no longer be a burden on your shoulders. Now serve the Lord your God and His people Israel" (2 Chronicles 35:3).

The verb *put* in this verse may be a clue that the Ark was not in the Temple. If the Ark was already resting in the Temple, why would Josiah ask the priests to put it there? When he says, "It shall no longer be a burden on your shoulders," this may indicate that the Ark was being carried from place to place. At least it seems to indicate that the Ark was outside the Temple, and probably outside Jerusalem. The final clue in this verse is interesting because it admonishes the priests to "serve the Lord . . . and His people

Israel." Why were the Levites asked to serve *their* God and the people of Israel? Had the Ark been taken someplace other than Israel?

Only two kings reigned between Hezekiah and Josiah:
Manasseh (687–642 BC) and Amon (642–640 BC), who was assas-
sinated after only two years as king. Manasseh, who had a long and
wicked reign, will always be remembered as a king who did evil in
the sight of the Lord. He is the person most likely responsible for
allowing the Ark of the Covenant to slip away from Solomon's
Temple. Manasseh is the perfect villain in this ancient mystery:

> *He rebuilt the high places which Hezekiah his father had
> destroyed; he raised up altars for Baal, and made a
> wooden image, as Ahab king of Israel had done; and he
> worshiped all the host of heaven and served them. He also
> built altars in the house of the Lord, of which the Lord had
> said, "In Jerusalem I will put My name." And he built al-
> tars for all the host of heaven in the two courts of the house
> of the Lord. Also he made his son pass through the fire,
> practiced soothsaying, used witchcraft, and consulted spir-
> itists and mediums. He did much evil in the sight of the
> Lord, to provoke Him to anger. He even set a carved im-
> age of Asherah that he had made, in the house of which the
> Lord had said to David and to Solomon his son, "In this
> house and in Jerusalem, which I have chosen out of all the
> tribes of Israel, I will put My name forever"....Moreover
> Manasseh shed very much innocent blood, till he had filled
> Jerusalem from one end to another, besides his sin by
> which he made Judah sin, in doing evil in the sight of the
> Lord. (2 Kings 21:3-7, 16)*

As a result of Manasseh's loathsome actions, God pronounced a grave sentence on Israel. He removed his hand from Israel—and very likely the Ark was removed as well.

I believe that the loyal priests would have risked their lives to protect the Ark from the evil king. The Levites stood against kings who dared to trifle with the sanctity of the Ark. In one instance, King Uzziah burned incense on the incense altar and the priests literally threw him out of the Temple (see 2 Chronicles 26). There is no doubt that when Manasseh put pagan idols alongside the Ark of the Covenant in the Holy of Holies, the priests would have been repulsed and would have somehow hidden the Ark to avoid its defilement.

The Bible gives subtle clues that the Ark may have been taken to Egypt. In 2 Chronicles 35, we are told that Josiah prepared the Temple (even though, I believe, the Ark was gone), and in the same passage, Josiah went out to fight Neco, the pharaoh of Egypt. Josiah had no clear reason to do so. Neco had sent messengers warning Josiah to stay away and leave him alone.

Neco's ambassadors said, "What do you want with me, king of Judah? I have no quarrel with you today! I am on my way to fight another nation, and God has told me to hurry! Do not interfere with God, who is with me, or he will destroy you" (2 Chronicles 35:21, NLT).

A close look reveals that, in this instance at least, Pharaoh was taking orders directly from the God of Israel.

In effect, Pharaoh Neco scolded Josiah, saying, "Refrain from meddling with God, who is with me, lest he destroy you" (v. 21). In Hebrew, the statement doesn't just mean "God is on my side." Rather, the preposition indicates that God was literally with Neco, physically in his company. In a dramatic statement that goes almost unnoticed in the Bible, Neco informs Josiah that the God of the Hebrews is with him, personally on-site! This amazing bit of dialogue reveals two crucial points: Neco had received his orders directly from God, and God was somehow actually present with Neco.

In times past, both of these statements had been made of Israel—but only when the Ark traveled with the nation. With the Ark in front of Israel's armies, God had led his people into battle, speaking to them from between the cherubim. Could Neco be claiming something that could only be true if he were in possession of the Ark and the mercy seat? Was God actually *with* Neco, relaying orders from the Ark?

Josiah refused to heed Neco's warning and even disguised himself. The account states, "But Josiah refused to listen to Neco, to whom God had indeed spoken, and he would not turn back. Instead, he led his army into battle on the plain of Megiddo" (2 Chronicles 35:22, NLT).

It is quite possible that Josiah simply could not stomach the thought that Israel's Ark of the Covenant was in Pharaoh's hands. He had to fight Pharaoh to get it back. But just as Neco had forewarned, Josiah died in the battle.

The statement that Josiah "refused to listen to Neco, to whom God had indeed spoken" (v. 22, NLT) is not a quote from Neco but from the scribe who wrote 2 Chronicles, who states that Neco was receiving his instructions directly from the mouth of God (or God's manifest presence). God had spoken to Moses from above the mercy seat, and he may have spoken to Neco in the same way.

This tragic event in Josiah's life may provide a clue that the Ark had been taken into Egypt by priests fleeing the atrocities of

Manasseh. It is entirely possible that during Josiah's reign, the Ark and the mercy seat were in Neco's care. It is also conceivable that Josiah's purpose in confronting Neco was to take the Ark back by force—even though God had made it clear that Jerusalem and the Temple would be destroyed. If these things are true, then the Ark remained safely with the Egyptians rather than becoming part of the plunder when Nebuchadnezzar sacked Jerusalem thirteen years later.   *God usually used Egypt as refuge/city.*

If the Ark was gone from the Temple during Josiah's reign so that Nebuchadnezzar couldn't have taken it to Babylon as other legends suggest, the best option for tracking the Ark, in my opinion, was to pursue the idea that it was taken to Elephantine Island on the Nile River, as the Ethiopian monks had told me. I needed to go there to continue my search.

TO ELEPHANTINE ISLAND IN EGYPT

The young Egyptian hoisted the fluttering sails of the felucca, and its sleek low hull glided from the dock and across the Nile to Elephantine Island. This was the fastest sailboat in Egypt, and its owner, though youthful in appearance, had won the famous felucca sailboat race up the Nile. This gave him local hero status and the honor of being first in line to take waiting tourists across the wide river to the archaeological ruins on the island.

The Nile's meandering current cuts a swath through the desert and divides its flow around the small island of Elephantine. A ten-minute sail in the freshly painted felucca took me across the Nile to the island's rocky edge as gulls circled overhead. Wide, hand-cut steps led to a concrete museum among several acres of ancient ruins. The museum was stuffy and smelled of the ancient artifacts on display. They did not interest me. I wanted to know about an old wooden box with gold overlay that might have been here more than two thousand years ago.

A Muslim woman with a black silk scarf tied around her face sat behind a desk. She smiled warmly, and I asked, "Can anyone tell me about the Ark of the Covenant ever being on this island?"

She tilted her head, perhaps surprised by the unusual question. After a short moment she said softly, "I will get for you Dr. Hanna."

She walked to the door of an office and spoke to whoever was inside, then pointed at me. A small Egyptian man in his forties emerged from the office.

"Yes, what is your question, please?" His tone was formal.

"I was wondering if you could tell me if the Ark of the Covenant has ever been on this island."

He held out his hand and said, "Let me introduce myself. I am Dr. Atif Hanna with the Institute of Cairo Coptic Studies."

I introduced myself and explained that I was researching the history of the Ark of the Covenant. "Do you know anything about the Ark? Was it ever on this island?"

Dr. Hanna said nothing but waved for me to follow him. We left the museum and strolled up a dirt path to a rounded hilltop. Tunnels honeycombed the area, and toppled statues and columns littered the ground.

Dr. Hanna sat down on a carved rock. He looked skyward, apparently netting his thoughts, then gave a short dissertation in an Egyptian accent as thick as tar.

"The Ark of the Covenant moved from Jerusalem at the time of King Manasseh and came to Elephantine Island. Yes, the Ark of the Covenant remained here for some time at the Jewish temple. In the third century before Christ, some of the Jewish community moved south to Abyssinia or Ethiopia, and the Ark of the Covenant is still until now in that area."

He then told me about papyrus scrolls that were written by Hebrews in Aswan to those in Jerusalem in the mid-seventh century before Christ. The writings referred to the "temple of Yahweh" used to shelter the "Person of God." Dr. Hanna said that the Hebrews built a replica temple on the island about 650 BC during the reign of Judah's King Manasseh, and hostile Egyptians destroyed it. Perhaps the Jewish sacrifice of rams was one reason for this, because the ram was the image of an Egyptian god. After two hundred years, in approximately 410 BC, the whole Hebrew community mysteriously vanished.

I already knew that some scholars believed that the community on Elephantine consisted of Hebrew mercenaries; others thought it was a mix of refugees, including Levitical priests seeking sanctuary from the wicked King Manasseh's persecution.

Could this Elephantine temple have been modeled after the First Temple in Jerusalem? Was it a temporary resting place for the Ark? Although building such a temple on Egyptian soil would have been a serious violation of Israelite law, which forbade constructing a temple or offering sacrifices outside of Jerusalem, it may have been rationalized because of Manasseh's evil excesses. In any event, the Elephantine Hebrews clearly thought that Yahweh had resided physically in their temple. A number of papyri speak of Yahweh as "dwelling" there.[8] And if such a temple was built to house the Ark, it helped to explain the Ark's disappearance from Jerusalem in the early-to-mid-600s BC and why it didn't arrive in Ethiopia until approximately 470 BC.

Had the Levites taken the Ark to Elephantine Island and placed it in a replica temple built especially to house it? And when Egyptian goodwill crumbled two hundred years later, did they then proceed south to Ethiopia and hide the Ark on T'ana Kirkos?

Dr. Hanna said that in 525 BC, a Persian king invaded Egypt and destroyed many Egyptian temples, but he did not touch a stone on the Jewish temple at Elephantine. The invader's name was Cambyses, and his father was Cyrus the Great, the king who ordered that building begin on the Second Temple in Jerusalem.

"The Ark was never mentioned in the Bible again," Dr. Hanna said, "because it came here to the Jewish temple at Elephantine."

The Jewish refugees constructed a temple whose dimensions and appearance—exterior pillars, gateways of stone, roof of cedar wood—were modeled precisely after Solomon's Temple. Papyrus records indicate that the Hebrews performed ritual animal sacrifices at the Elephantine temple just as in Jerusalem, including the all-important sacrifice of a lamb during Passover.

The Elephantine temple of Yahweh was destroyed in 410 BC, within sixty years of the date that legend says the Ark arrived in Ethiopia (around 470 BC).

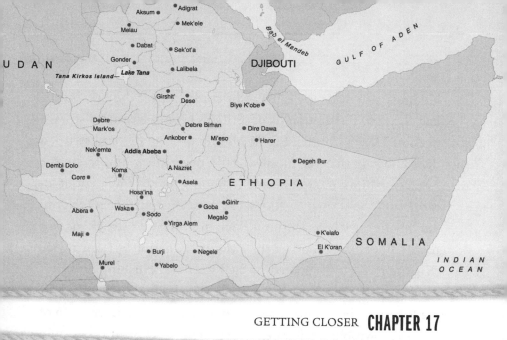

Aksum, Ethiopia, 2000

In April 2000 I led a research team across the Sinai Peninsula, re-tracing the Exodus of Moses. We filmed the proposed route from the Nile Delta to the tip of Sinai in Egypt. Four of the team members suggested a quick side trip to Ethiopia to visit Aksum and then a day trip to T'ana Kirkos Island. Because we were so close, it seemed like a good idea.

In Aksum I met a man named Haile who boldly claimed that he could enter Saint Mary of Zion Church and obtain a detailed description of the various objects sequestered in the treasury there. Normally I would have dismissed such a brash claim, but Haile was the curator of the Aksum Museum and had by government permission enjoyed yearly access to Saint Mary of Zion to catalog their holdings. He made it clear that he could not see the Ark, but he had access to the thousands of artifacts kept in basement storage in Saint Mary's Church. I took him up on his offer and struck a deal, knowing that the monks would never allow him to see the Ark. I gave him a modest payment, hoping for any fragment of information about what lay hidden in those dusty archives. I felt uneasy about the whole venture, which in some ways struck me as a payoff. But Haile smoothed the awkward situation by assuring me that the monks—decimated by civil wars and crushing poverty—would benefit from the extra revenue. The long-term plan was for me to return the following year and hear a detailed description of the unknown objects in the chapel archives. Hopefully, I would also learn more about the gold object secluded within the thick walls of Saint Mary of Zion.

STORMY WEATHER

The following day our team flew to Bahar Dar and chartered a rusty-hulled government boat to tour several islands on Lake T'ana. Misgana, my guide from the last trip, was with us. It was good to see him again.

It was early afternoon when we left the dock. The jade-green waters were flat, and it looked like another beautiful day in Africa. It was supposed to be a quick turnaround trip. We had a much bigger boat this time, and even though it was battered, it seemed to make good time. We stayed longer on T'ana Kirkos than planned. I always enjoy visiting with Abba and the monks, and the team snapped away, getting photos of what most of them described as the most uniquely amazing place they had ever seen.

As usual, we brought medicine, and team member Dr. Pete

Leininger treated the monks who had new maladies. Dr. Pete said that if they only had clean water and soap, they could avoid 90 percent of their current medical problems. When we left the island, it was later than the captain had planned, and when I asked him to pilot us to the dense jungle island of Daga Stephanos, he was miffed. I gave him some extra money, and he grumbled and steered our new course.

Ethiopians regard Daga Stephanos as one of the holiest places on the sacred lake. Monks have maintained a church monastery there for the past one thousand years, and the island houses the tombs of five former Ethiopian emperors. Their glass-encased crypts are in a cave high on a cliff. I had heard from monks on T'ana Kirkos that there were ancient writings there, and I wanted to have a look. Serendipity might offer up some interesting clues.

Daga Stephanos was a dark, eerie place. The monks wore hoods, ate in private, and never smiled. Our short stay was uncomfortable, and we felt we were not welcome.

The captain seemed skittish as the day went on, sensing something that we missed about the lake's unpredictable temperament. After being on Daga Stephanos for about an hour, he ordered us to get back to the boat. The sun was about to set.

"Hurry! Hurry!" he barked. He began to pull up anchor. "Come now! Come now!" We scrambled down the flinty cliffs that spilled out onto the small rocky lagoon where the boat was anchored. I could see the captain's face, glistening with beads of sweat. He continued to shout, "We go! We go!"

We tossed our backpacks on board, and the captain wasted no time in giving the old boat full throttle. The clattering engine belched plumes of black smoke out bent exhaust pipes as we headed across open water. I noticed that the captain kept turning around and looking behind him as if something were pursuing him. I turned to see what it was.

A massive bank of black, angry clouds rose on the horizon. A boiling jungle storm was on our heels. It was soon clear that we would not be able to outrun it. Although the captain pressed the boat to its limits, the storm was moving faster than we were. I could do nothing but watch.

Foaming swells began to pound the hull. Minutes later those same swells grew until they crashed over the deck of the dilapi-dated vessel and returned to the churning lake in white, frothy streams. Surging, white-capped waves threw mist into the air, and a driving wind pelted us with stinging spray. The boat heeled from side to side.

The lake might as well have been an ocean—it was every bit as menacing. Our lives were riding on diesel-powered driftwood. Night was held off only a short distance by our cabin lights. The wind grew more violent as purple-green waves crashed over the railings, shrieking as if consumed by pain or madness.

After one violent blast, Misgana staggered over the rolling deck to inform me that from his experience, the worst of the storm lay ahead. That wasn't the news I wanted to hear.

"What can we do?" I asked.

Misgana gave me a courageous smile and said, "Hold on."

Misgana's words were prophetic. I was holding on when a shud-der ran through the boat, and we heard metal shredding. The boat's forward momentum came to a brutal stop, and we all went sprawl-ing across the wet deck, bags and duffels skipping alongside.

A new sound emerged as the spinning rotor clattered against a rock. A few moments later, we realized that the propeller had snapped off. Our captain screamed into his radio. I struggled up from the deck. The crew's reactions ran the gamut from stunned surprise to utter terror.

Swimming for our lives seemed a distinct necessity. In the inky waves, the captain had run the boat aground in the tricky narrows just off the port of Bahar Dar. So close and yet so far! The captain couldn't see to steer clear of the rocks.

I felt responsible. I had insisted on the side trip to Daga Stephanos, and now our boat was disabled with no help in sight. Our five-man crew scrambled for the two life vests on board. Misgana spoke to me over the wind, "I will not swim to shore. I grew up on this lake. I know what lives in the water. There are crocodiles and hippos along the shore and big snakes in the jungle. No, I won't swim!"

"What are you going to do?" I asked.

"I prefer a pleasant death. I will go down with the boat."

Lightning flashed. Thunder echoed along the water, adding its voice to the wind. The skipper kept gunning the engine, hoping somehow to free us from the reef.

The captain powered the engines again, but it no longer mattered. The propeller shaft had sheared off at the stem. It spun uselessly, unable to bite into the sea. The engine spewed dark clouds of smoke as the pilot kept pumping the throttle and bellowing into his radio, and then the cabin lights went out.

Ray Ardizonne, a team member and a man of deep faith, shouted over the wind, "Let's go below and pray!" Ray, a retired air force colonel, was a trusted friend with a steady hand in the face of danger. It was the best idea anyone had come up with, so we struggled down the steps into the leaking cabin, where we starting praying with passion.

"Dear Father, help us!" Ray shouted over the racket.

Dr. Pete Leininger chimed in, "Lord, we don't know what to do. But we trust you to get us to shore safely."

The boat had heeled farther into the water. Blinding bolts of lightning crashed overhead, ripping the sky as the boat thrashed against the rocks. I imagined the ship's metal skin splitting open.

Misgana approached with unbelievable calm, saying, "The captain can't raise anyone on the radio, and we are still three and a half miles from shore."

Three and a half miles is a long way to swim in calm water. In this boiling lake it would be impossible. We were stuck with the boat as surely as the boat was stuck on the rocks. If the boat went under, the chances of any of us making it to shore were slim to none.

There was another flash, but it was pale and close to the water. And it was moving.

I saw a yellow-white light flickering in the distant swells. I kept my eyes on the light as it approached with excruciating slowness. Fifteen minutes later, an open-hulled skiff emerged, its occupants fighting furiously against the gale. These fishermen had seen our cabin lights bobbing in the narrows. Dressed in rubber boots and rain slickers and navigating their fragile fifteen-foot fishing craft filled with nets and floats, they finally maneuvered near enough to our craft that we could climb on. Their small boat strained and rolled with the wind, propelled by an antiquated, five-horsepower outboard engine. We had been stranded for two hours when they arrived, and no strangers ever looked so good!

When we clambered aboard the fishing boat, our combined

weight pressed the small boat deep into the churning water. The five-horse outboard went back to work.

It took half an hour to make the three-plus miles to a rickety dock at the port of Bahar Dar. Waterlogged and rain-whipped, we were tired but still intact, with cause for rejoicing. It was one of many close calls through the years. Once on the dock, Ray and Pete began pressing wads of birr into the fishermen's hands, not knowing how else to thank them.

We invited our proud rescuers to join us for lunch the next afternoon at our hotel. They arrived together, dressed in the best clothes they owned. Their frayed shirts, washed and pressed by their wives, were buttoned to the top, and their stubbled faces were now shaved smooth. However, the hotel staff didn't want poor, common fishermen in their hotel, and they forcibly stopped them from entering the lobby. When we saw this, we confronted the hotel manager, making it clear that he had better reconsider this policy. Ten minutes later we were enjoying a lavish lunch. We treated our honored guests as heroic angels of mercy, and they left smiling, their pockets bulging with our remaining birr.

I couldn't stop thinking about Haile and the payment I had given him a couple of days earlier in Aksum. I was worried that buying this information might not be right. On the face of it, it seemed a simple business deal in which no one would be harmed. But the shipwreck had started me thinking. I was feeling the same as I had when I was sneaking up Mount Sinai, and I hated it. Was I again stretching the boundaries, pushing the unclear line between aggressive research and trespass? Haile had said that everything was fine, but still soggy from our mishap, I was rethinking that. Was our near disaster at sea a warning to prevent me from peering behind the veil of the chapel in Aksum? I dismissed the idea as paranoia and as unresolved fear from the previous night. Haile had said it was okay, and I would leave it at that—for now.

TIMKAT IN AKSUM

Nearly a year later, I was flying back to Ethiopia with a small group to visit the president of Ethiopia. Behind me sat Mary Irwin, and under her seat was a flat black carrying case containing an Ethiopian flag that had gone to the moon with Jim on Apollo 15. She was going to present the flag to the president of Ethiopia. The other members of the team were my brother Paul; our good friends Daniel and Carol Ayres; board member Pete Leininger and his wife, Barbara; writer David Halbrook; and cameraman Brian Boorujy.

Before we visited the president, we would first go to Aksum for their famed Timkat (baptism of Christ) celebration. After a bumpy flight, we touched down on the newly paved Aksum runway. The airport now had a terminal, a big improvement from when Joby and I first bounced down the rutted runway filled with sheep, camels, and cows.

"Welcome to Aksum," I told the group.

Our chartered bus arrived, and the driver collected our bags and drove us straight into Aksum. "We need to hurry," I told them, aware that the Timkat festival, under way since dawn, would heighten in an hour or so.

I told the driver to skip the hotel and take us directly to the main square. Minutes later, he deposited us near a huge fig tree at the edge of a massive gathering.

Timkat is the most highly celebrated religious holiday in Ethiopia. Priests and monks dress in ornate, brightly colored robes. Their nonclerical attendants wear the traditional white cotton shawls called *shemmas* or the thicker woolen cloaks called *gebbis*. The faithful walk for days and even weeks from villages all over the countryside to attend Timkat. This celebration can be a wild and robust spectacle or a deeply solemn ceremony. We could hear singing from the center of the crowd, and I sensed that we had arrived just in time.

Aksum's leading patriarchs, dressed in traditional white robes and black shoulder capes, leaned on tall prayer sticks and swayed to the deep throb of the *kebero* (a large oval drum with a leather head stretched over a wooden frame). Feminine voices chanted an ancient Ge'ez hymn, and the jingle of silver-plated *sistra* filled the silences between the *kebero* beats. Here and there, the deacons raised their *sistras* in unison, letting them fall in a clear, musical jangle.

At a distance stood a group of slender, bearded priests, robed in green silk and red *k'oba* (skullcaps). They stood near the tree trunk, holding the festival's centerpiece and spiritual totem—a red, jewel-encrusted box *(tabot)*—over their heads. Inside the box is a replica of the Ark of the Covenant (or the Ten Commandments, depending on who you ask). Not so long ago, the original Ark was supposedly wrapped in the same ornamental cloth and paraded through the streets, but today's priests make it clear that they are holding a ceremonial substitute and not the Ark.

The celebration centers on the baptism of Christ but features Levite costumes. Costly robes are bound by gilded *k'enat* (belts), and one can admire the high priest's girdle, the tight-fitting *k'oba* or mitre, and his glittering *askema* (scapular).

From the low throb and the light jingle of the *kebero* and *sistra*, the energy began to build. Individuals in the crowd began bouncing rhythmically on their toes while playing flutes, fiddles, lyres, or harps. One group of men thrust ceremonial prayer sticks and *sistras* toward the sky. A cheer erupted like a war chant, and a shrill burst from the women pierced the hot afternoon air: *"Ell-ell-ell-ell-ell-ell."*

At once, the square shook with the sound and motion of exuberant patrons. Their constantly moving feet kicked dust into the air. From under the shade tree, surrounded by a phalanx of silk-robed patriarchs, the priest holding the *tabot* suddenly set out, inciting a burst of stamping feet and frenzied shouts. The crowd engulfed our team and swept us along in the procession. We were scattered among troupes of dancers that whirled, jumped, and shouted to the rhythms of the young men pounding drums. It was the most physical worship I had ever experienced.

With each step, the crowd swelled, swallowing up spectators—small children, the elderly, the lame, sick, and dying, the happy and healthy. All were keeping an eye on the raised *tabot*, as if the Ark were leading them into battle. We hustled past the ancient walls and altars of the Saint Mary of Zion monastery grounds, past the castles and fortified cathedrals, past the arched windows and stonework facades of the monastery churches, past the tall bell tower with its Arabic globes and astrological symbols to arrive, finally, in a leaping, twirling, quivering mob at the front gate of the holy chapel of the Ark.

The crowd pooled near the iron fence, building its energy as the lurching multitude reached a crescendo. At the front of the crowd, a young man, savagely beating his *kebero*, led a troupe of priestly dancers who leaped, shouted, and clapped their hands with otherworldly intensity. The wall of sound swelled with trumpet blasts, frenzied chanting, and the haunting thrum of dozens of ten-stringed *begegna*. A dervish dressed in a white cotton robe whirled before the priests, who marched in place to grant the pilgrims a last glimpse of the sacred *tabot*.

The festival must have resembled the wild scene captured in Scripture three thousand years ago, when David and the house of Israel brought the Ark of the Lord to the gates of Jerusalem. "David and all the people of Israel were celebrating before the Lord, singing songs and playing all kinds of musical instruments—lyres, harps, tambourines, castanets, and cymbals. . . . So David and all the people of Israel brought up the Ark of the Lord with shouts of joy and the blowing of rams' horns" (2 Samuel 6:5, 15, NLT).

Gradually, the music softened and the dancers settled. The crowd still chanted as the priests slowly circled and entered the rear gate of the chapel with the *tabot*. I skirted the crowd just in time to see them march up the stairs and into the church, disappearing into the precise place from which the Guardian, also know as the *Atang*, had emerged a year earlier. That the Guardian never appeared supported the *tabot*'s purely ceremonial function.

The music and dancing soon abated. The energy drained from the crowd, and an eerie silence fell on Aksum as the people dispersed. My team gathered at the bus, amazed at what they had just seen. We rode up the hill to the Yeha Hotel in silence, each of us lost in our thoughts.

Haile stood in the lobby waiting for me. He greeted me as I descended from the bus, then pulled me aside and whispered, "I have seen it. I have seen the Ark."

A STOLEN GLIMPSE

David Halbrook and I quickly led our Ethiopian friend to the stone terrace behind the hotel restaurant, and I said, "Haile, tell us what you saw."

Without hesitating, Haile told us that he, accompanied by two monks, had sneaked into the secret chamber where the Ark is sheltered. He described the Ark, its general size and appearance closely matching the biblical description of a wooden box covered with gold, its shape and dimensions well within known specifications. Of course, anyone in Ethiopia could have told us as much. Haile, like every grade-schooler in Aksum, had known those passages from his youth.

"Now, Haile," I continued, "tell us about the cherubim above the mercy seat. Exactly how are they positioned?"

With hands tracing shapes in the air, he said, "The angels had the faces of men, with their bodies stationed over the Ark."

"What did the wings look like, Haile?"

Halbrook handed his notepad to Haile, who began sketching a rough drawing. We leaned in to watch as he drew two angels facing each other. Neither stood upright like a statue, as is so often depicted. Instead, they appeared with heads bowed, facing the top of the gold box. Haile then drew wings that resembled feathery arms, reverently extended to overshadow the Ark. It was a rough drawing, but seemed to approximate cherubim fashioned from hammered gold.

Glancing at me out of the corner of his eye, Halbrook asked, "Haile, are you sure this is what the wings looked like?"

"Yes," he said. Then without prompting, he added, "As you can see, the wings could be where someone might sit. The mercy seat is a type of chair."

Haile then told us how he had entered the chapel in the company of two monks who assisted the *Atang*. The story then took a weird turn, and I didn't know whether to believe it or not.

Haile said that he and the two monks had entered the church of the Ark under the official authority of cataloging some of the thousands of history books, crosses, crowns, paintings, and manuscripts stored in the chapel's treasury basement.

Haile's voice grew dark as he explained how he and the two monks had left the storage chamber and walked slowly upstairs, through several heavily reinforced wooden doors, until they reached the outer chamber of the inner sanctum where the monks kept the Ark. Haile was now speaking in jumbled English so softly that we could barely hear him. He said that they had entered into the Most Holy Place, where in the darkness they could barely see a large stone chamber sitting on top of a stone pedestal, like a mausoleum vault, approximately five feet long and four feet high. The top of the structure was gabled, like the roof of a house.

"Where was the Guardian?" Halbrook asked. "Isn't he the only one who ever sees the holy relic? How did you and these monks get past the Guardian into the inner sanctum?"

"We are allowed because of my appointment as a government official of the museum," Haile said with authority. "Once a year I am obliged to inventory all the items in the church treasury."

Haile insisted that he was given permission because of his affiliation with the Aksum museum, but I had my doubts. I knew he was not allowed to see the object believed to be the Ark. A more likely explanation, if he saw the Ark at all, was that he sneaked into the chamber of the Ark and peered into holy darkness with a shaking candle in hand. Or maybe Haile was lying through his teeth in hopes of getting more money from me.

"Okay, Haile," I sighed. "Once you entered the inner sanctuary, what did you do? What happened?"

"It was very dark," he replied. "One of the monks and I walked over and began to open up the stone vault housing the Ark. It was very heavy and hard to move. Once we slid it from its position, we noticed that there was a silver box inside, an ornate hand-engraved lining that surrounded and protected the Ark." Several moments later he added, "We saw the Ark then . . . and then we must have fallen down, for when I opened my eyes, we all lay on the floor. We lay there, unable to move. We had to be carried out by some monks."

"What?" I was having trouble believing what I had heard. "What happened to the monks, the two men who were with you?"

"Three weeks ago one of the monks died," he answered. "It was from the Ark. Tomorrow, if you like, we will visit his grave."

"What about the other monk?" Halbrook asked.

"He is very sick and can no longer continue his work at the chapel. He has been forced to retire. He can barely stand. It seems his body is dying."

My search was now hurtling into the surreal. I had no idea what to believe. Had they actually seen the Ark or what they believed to be the Ark? Had the very thought of the Ark's power, magnified by a lifetime of potent religious indoctrination, overwhelmed their guilty consciences? Had those two men been frightened to death?

For several long moments we sat there on the breezy terrace, saying nothing. Haile finally broke the silence. "I must go now," he said. I was taken off guard when he returned an expensive camera I had given him. He also offered to give back the money. It was as if he were trying to distance himself from what he had done, from the money, and from me. I had seen fear before, and this man had it.

I saw no point in pressing the interrogation. I would probably never really know what had happened with Haile and those monks, and my own thoughts had become muddled. Halbrook nodded and looked just as surprised and confused as I was. We escorted Haile down to the lobby.

Haile walked slowly down the road and vanished into the night.

All along I had felt that getting information from the monks about the Ark was like digging through concrete with a plastic spoon. Now we were getting what I thought was too much, too weird, and too fast. I didn't know what to think. It did seem certain that we had one dead monk and one hovering at death's threshold. Was this an unfortunate coincidence mixed with the active imaginations of frightened, fragile old men? Fully understanding all the dynamics was probably impossible. The whole strange matter might have to remain in the long line of unanswered mysteries, but such mysteries in Ethiopia had ceased to surprise me.

Most Ethiopians have a holy fear and an adoring worship for whatever is in that church. Since childhood, they have been taught that the gold box in the church of Saint Mary of Zion is the true Ark of the Covenant made at Mount Sinai. They know that it was carried through the wilderness, placed in the Temple by Solomon, and now resides with them. They see themselves as the custodians of this divine relic, and they believe that the wrath of the Almighty will fall on them if they fail in that responsibility.

The next day I took Haile up on his offer to visit the monk's grave. I took several witnesses, and there I met the brother of the deceased monk, who told me the story exactly as Haile had described it.

I interviewed the second old monk with several witnesses gathered around me. He described the Ark exactly as Haile had. Days after that interview, I heard that the old monk had died.

BAD THINGS DO HAPPEN

The Bible tells us that the Ark could become an object of powerful retribution if not treated with proper respect. The Scriptures list a very specific protocol for its care and transport. When these divinely assigned ordinances have been violated in the past, the result has been tragedy and death. The sons of Aaron died in the presence of the Ark, many died from just looking in it, and Uzzah died when he tried to steady it on an oxcart during improper transport (2 Samuel 6:6-7). The Ethiopian Christians read the Bible repeatedly, especially the parts that relate to the care of the Ark and its strict observances. They respect its power.

After Haile's account, I needed to be alone to get my balance back after this unsettling course of events. I walked down a narrow dirt path bathed in the light of a ripening moon and stopped to watch a gathering of women with long white shawls draped over their heads. They read from their Bibles in the flickering light of slender candles. Distant drums thumped a barely audible rhythm in the darkness, and the haunting melody of a solo flute floated above the town.

I walked among a group of people sitting around a roaring fire that cast swirling sparks heavenward. The people of Aksum had come to know me, and many had received medicine on my many journeys to see them. As I walked up the road, I passed several black faces, but I couldn't make out a single feature in the shadows of their shawls except the white of their eyes and teeth. Despite the dirt, the dung, and the flies, I loved being there.

As I trudged along, a thin man emerged from the darkness. He had a brown shawl wrapped tightly around his face. I couldn't make out his identity until we moved into the road, where a faint light from a nearby fire cast an orange glow across his face. It was a young deacon from the church named Godefa. He was a well-respected church leader who might one day be the Administrator of the Ark of the Covenant. He smiled, putting his hand out to mine. He held it tightly, then hugged me in the traditional side-to-side, cheek-to-cheek greeting. He said nothing, but I sensed that he knew everything.

He caught me off guard with his embrace. I had seen this man follow the *tabot* to Saint Mary of Zion Church. He was the one beating the big zebra-skin drum at the front of the procession.

He whispered, "Tell me, Mr. Bob. Why do you come here to Aksum?"

Suspecting that he was referring to the debacle with Haile, I stammered, "I am looking for information about the lost Ark of the Covenant."

He placed his shawl about his kind face, smiled, and bowed as if he were leaving. I was glad he was going, for the interview with Haile still troubled me. Perhaps it is more accurate to say that I felt guilty. But Godefa didn't leave. Instead, he asked sagely, "Why do you look for something that will never be yours?"

I had no answer. I could only stare.

He studied me for a moment, then asked another question. "And why do you try to find something that has never been lost?"

He bowed, turned, and walked up the winding path toward Saint Mary of Zion Church, his form soon fading into the blue shadows.

At that moment I decided never again to try to peer behind the veil. I did not want to pry, dig, or use aggressive investigative skills to find out what the Ark looked like. I would not try to get drawings or pictures or descriptive accounts of the object they possessed. They just may be the keepers of the Ark, and if they are, they will remain so until the appointed hour of God.

The monks do not care if the world believes them or not; their indifference is limitless. I think they hope that the world doesn't believe them because they want to be left alone. But Westerners want answers. We want proof, and we demand an accounting for their claim that they have the Ark. They never promoted the idea in the first place; Graham Hancock and I, as well as many other people, have done that. I was in the mix of promoters, and I regretted it. I felt that I had crossed the blurred line of research and had stepped on a sacred garment. At that moment, I decided I would somehow help the young deacon to protect the gold-covered wooden box in that chapel. It was a year before I realized how important my decision was.

AT THE PRESIDENTIAL PALACE

Two long, maroon Mercedes sedans were sent by the Ethiopian National Palace to retrieve us from the Sheraton Addis early one Saturday. On this morning of our last full day in Ethiopia, Mary Irwin would present President Negaso Gidada with a framed Ethiopian tricolor flag, the one that had traveled with her husband to the moon.

The president's personal chauffeurs picked us up and drove us the twenty minutes across town, slowing down as we approached the faded gray-marble pillars and iron-spiked gates of the National Palace. Three armed guards in camouflage fatigues waved us in. We proceeded down a narrow, tree-lined lane and eased to a stop in front of a huge white building. A red carpet trailed down the palace steps to the sedans. We stepped out and followed it up into the palace, where butlers in double-breasted suits escorted us into the foyer, carpeted in red and dominated by an enormous tiger-skin rug with mouth agape. By any measure, this engagement was a climactic conclusion to our Ethiopian adventure.

I almost laughed. The pomp and ceremony, the chauffeurs and butlers, the gardens and lavish presidential trappings seemed an absurd contrast to my first visit to Ethiopia. When Joby and I were wandering the streets, we were fortunate to catch a cab, and we were staying in an inner-city fleabag hotel with cockroaches the size of my thumb. It would have seemed fantastic then to imagine that one day I'd lead a chauffeured U.S. delegation to these stately offices.

A palace steward appeared in the doorway and led us across the vestibule into a large reception hall. At the back of the room stood the president and his attendants; behind them was a semicircular gold-paneled divider inlaid with portraits of past emperors and girded at each end by elephant tusks the size of tall men. Mary Irwin stepped forward, cradling the framed Ethiopian flag carefully in her arms. It had been matted with an autographed picture of her husband standing on the moon beside the lunar module. The rest of us formed a tight line behind Mary.

President Negaso Gidada, a diminutive, bespectacled fellow with warm eyes and a light, upturned mustache, watched us from the back of the room. We approached slowly. Mary moved lightly toward the president, speaking slowly in a low, measured voice. She gracefully informed him that the Ethiopian flag she carried, emblazoned with the Lion of Judah, had been with her husband on the surface of the moon for three days and should be regarded as a gift of peace and brotherhood from the American people.

Seconds before her presentation, Mary had sliced her hand on the barbed metal edge of the picture frame, and now she shook hands with the president with a blood-splotched tissue pressed into her palm to constrict the blood flow. No one seemed to notice. The president received the gift as a "highly esteemed national treasure."

After the ceremony, Halbrook and I walked forward to stand beside the president. He caught our eye and greeted us warmly, appearing keen and alert to hear whatever we had to say. His first words praised Mary's short speech. He happily explained that his father had been a Presbyterian minister and one of the first in Ethiopia to learn Braille.

"I myself became a Christian when missionaries from Pennsylvania came over and witnessed to my father," he said proudly. "He got saved, and the rest of us followed."

"Ah," I said. "It is good to know we share a noble Savior." Aware that our time was short, I politely interjected, "Mr. President, my name is Bob Cornuke. I have spent the past seven years researching the Ark of the Covenant in Aksum."

At the mention of the Ark, the president's eyes lit up.

"Ah," he said. "Have you had the opportunity to meet the Guardian of the Ark?"

"Yes, sir," I replied. "I have met with the Guardian." I took a breath and added, "Mr. President, forgive me for being so bold, but may I ask—do *you* believe that the Ark lies in Aksum?"

He nodded and smiled. "I know it is—or should I say, I *believe* it is."

"How would you know that?" I asked.

He smiled. "I have ways of knowing. After all, I am the president."

I took that cryptic comment home to the States with me.

AN APPOINTMENT WITH THE ADMINISTRATOR

By January 2003, I had appeared on the *Ripley's Believe It or Not* television show, coauthored a book on the Ark with my good friend David Halbrook, and spoken all over the country on radio shows and in churches. I encountered a growing number of people who wanted to go to Ethiopia for an adventure. They wanted the thrill that searching for the Ark could bring. We had thirty excited people crammed into a bus and headed for the January 18 Timkat celebration. It was its usual wild ceremony, with masses of pilgrims celebrating the model of the Ark as priests carried it through the town amid screaming and singing throngs.

After Timkat was over and Aksum was quiet, I walked alone to Saint Mary of Zion Church. The Guardian was strolling around the perimeter in a yellow robe, swishing at flies with a clump of horsehairs woven on a stick. He nodded politely before sliding behind the faded red curtain stretched across the entry door that led to the chamber where I supposed that the Ark was kept.

After some time alone, I walked back to the Yeha Hotel, and the young deacon Godefa greeted me with a handshake and a hug. Then he whispered, "You are requested to see Narud. He saw you at Timkat and wanted to have you as a guest in his home."

I was stunned. No one had ever been invited to the home of the Administrator of the Ark. I stammered a yes and agreed to meet the following night.

As night fell the next day, a car pulled up to the Yeha Hotel. Godefa stepped out, and without a word, my friend and travel companion Dr. Chuck Missler and I got into the car. It traveled down a rutted road. Chuck is a PhD and has had a thirty-year career of developing high technology enterprises. He has also been the senior analyst for think tanks in the intelligence community. He is a biblical scholar and an expert in prophecy. I needed his presence at this meeting. What I was about to tell Narud would cause a stir

We came to a nondescript, mud-brick home and walked up a short path to a courtyard, where a tiny young woman wrapped in a blue shawl greeted us. She must have bowed ten times before waving us on to a room off the courtyard while shooing two scrawny chickens from the doorway. The room was small and dark, with three chairs and a bed crammed inside. The walls were of earth, with two brightly colored baskets as their only decoration. It was the room of a priest, a man born to a life of prayer, poverty, and obedience.

Narud stood and greeted us warmly. He wore a black robe and a regal-looking turban. We shook hands and were seated, after which Narud never moved except to swish away a fly with his horsehair swatter.

We sat in silence. After a few minutes, the tiny woman whom the church assigned to cook and care for Narud served popcorn in a colorful woven basket. Popcorn is the traditional food for guests in an Ethiopian home, followed by freshly roasted Ethiopian coffee.

The deacon finally broke the silence. "Narud met you several years ago; you brought medicine and money for us."

"I remember," I said. "It was an honor."

"Why do you come to Aksum?" Narud asked. Godefa translated.

I exhaled and said, "To learn about the Ark."

Narud looked at the deacon as if waiting for him to comment. When no comment came, Narud said, "We are the keepers of the Ark. We are poor. We have nothing but our faith and our devotion to the Ark." He stared at me with dark eyes, his words forged in wisdom and ripened with age.

He stroked his graying beard with his right hand, then continued. "We have nothing and that is why God chose us to have the Ark, to keep our eyes only on it, to protect it. It is all we have, and we will never allow the holy Ark to be taken away into a world that would soil its holiness."

Chuck looked over at me, wanting so much to say something. He knew, however, that a strict protocol is observed in this culture, deeply rooted in social mores established thousands of years ago. He handed me his Bible without saying a word and pointed to Isaiah 18 on the open page. I read the verses aloud, and Godefa translated. What we were about to tell Narud would be shocking. It had shocked me.

We laid out in detail a new theory that had come from a professor friend one spring morning at my Colorado Springs office. Questions had burned within me for years. Why Ethiopia? Why this country that is so far removed from the rest of the world? Why would God choose this chronically poor land to be the guardian for such a holy relic? And if the Ark does survive today, as the Ethiopians claim, then is there a reason for its continued existence?

Dr. Missler and I sat in the dark room of that humble house and shared our idea.

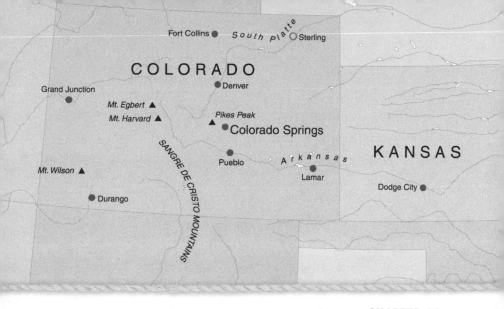

A THEORY EMERGES **CHAPTER 18**

Colorado Springs, 2001

I sat in my office in Colorado Springs enjoying a beautiful spring morning in the foothills of Pike's Peak. The columbines strained up through the newly thawed ground. The smell of pine sap filled the air and mixed with the scent of the loamy forest outside my open office window. Deer grazed in a nearby field.

I heard a car door slam and saw Ken Durham coming up the walk to my office. The bespectacled instructor with salt-and-pepper hair entered my office and sat down. Ken was assistant professor of biblical studies at a Christian college in Colorado. He had heard one of my radio interviews several months before about the Mount Sinai discovery. Like so many others, he took the initiative to contact me and suggested that we get together to exchange information regarding the Exodus.

Through the months, and in our conversations, I had barely mentioned my musings on the possibility that the Ark of the Covenant was in Ethiopia. One day I brought Ken a verse that I had been brooding over. I didn't know it at the time, but giving that verse to Ken would lead to an astonishing theory in biblical prophecy.

Isaiah 18 sounds like a travelogue of northern Ethiopia:

> *Woe to the land of whirring wings along the rivers of Cush, which sends envoys by sea in papyrus boats over the water. Go, swift messengers, to a people tall and smooth-skinned, to a people feared far and wide, an aggressive nation of strange speech, whose land is divided by rivers.*
>
> *At that time gifts will be brought to the Lord Almighty from a people tall and smooth-skinned, from a people feared far and wide, an aggressive nation of strange speech, whose land is divided by rivers—the gifts will be brought to Mount Zion, the place of the Name of the Lord Almighty. (Isaiah 18:1-2, 7, NIV)*

I recognized this verse as a prophecy about the ancient land of Ethiopia, although prophetic about *what*, I couldn't say. *Cush* is a Hebrew term for a nebulous territory that in the earliest Greek editions of the Bible was translated as "Ethiopia," and many new translations use *Ethiopia* instead of *Cush*. The Greek word for Ethiopia means "burnt faces," whereas the Hebrew term *Cush* refers to the entire Nile Valley south of Egypt, including Nubia and Abyssinia.[9] Today, most scholars agree that Cush applies only to the northern half of modern Ethiopia. It is from this land that Moses took a wife (Numbers 12:1).

I had considered these Isaiah 18 verses with particular interest. The rich imagery of papyrus boats and smooth-skinned natives seemed an accurate picture of the land I'd come to love. I knew Ethiopia as a place of "whirring wings" from my experience there with flies and mosquitoes. Cush's "papyrus boats" conjured up the Ethiopian *tankwas,* the papyrus canoes made by the shoreline natives of Lake T'ana even today. The native Ethiopians I had observed were indeed tall and smooth-skinned, with glowing, chestnut brown complexions. No one could dispute that it is a country "divided by rivers" that crisscross the mountainous land in the Horn of Africa. I had observed the roaring Atbara and Tekeze rivers cutting a glistening swath through hot, rocky highlands.

What, exactly, did Isaiah mean when he predicted that "at that time gifts will be brought to the Lord Almighty from a people tall and smooth-skinned. . . . The gifts will be brought to Mount Zion, the place of the Name of the Lord Almighty" (Isaiah 18:7, NIV)? It appeared from this verse that something prophetic would happen in Ethiopia that would directly impact Jerusalem, often referred to in Scripture as Mount Zion.

What gifts would the Ethiopians bring to the Lord?

Ken had been working on some other projects for me and had, at best, a casual knowledge of my interest in Ethiopia as the possible resting place of the Ark. In fact, he had mentioned that he did not believe the Ark could be in Ethiopia. As it turned out, however, that was about to change. The shift began when I pointed him to this verse and asked, "What do you make of it?"

Ken went into an explanation that set me back on my heels. "In

Isaiah 18, God is addressing the people who are beyond the rivers of Ethiopia. Moreover, Isaiah speaks of a procession traveling to Israel from Ethiopia following the second coming of Christ, when the Messiah returns triumphantly to establish his Kingdom on earth. Isaiah 18 is very clearly referring to the Day of the Lord, obviously a prophecy talking about a time in the future when Jesus will return."

Ken opened his Bible to a passage from the book of Ezekiel in which the prophet, in an angelic vision, saw and recorded the precise measurements, features, and configuration of the messianic Temple. Ezekiel's vision, almost obsessive in its painstaking detail, itemizes a sequence of events immediately following Christ's return. According to Ezekiel 43, Christ will rule from a messianic Temple in Jerusalem and take his place on a throne:

> *The glory of the Lord came into the temple by way of the gate which faces toward the east. The Spirit lifted me up and brought me into the inner court; and behold, the glory of the Lord filled the temple. Then I heard Him speaking to me from the temple, while a man stood beside me. And He said to me, "Son of man, this is the place of My throne and the place of the soles of My feet, where I will dwell in the midst of the children of Israel forever. No more shall the house of Israel defile My holy name." (Ezekiel 43:4-7)*

Ken continued to put forth his theory. "It seems straightforward. On that day, the Lord will come into his Temple and dwell with his people Israel forever. Yet, in an interesting twist, it also appears that Christ's own throne—'the place of the soles of My feet'—will reside within the messianic Temple. Never before in the Bible had another Hebrew king—David, Solomon, Josiah—ruled on a throne from inside the holy Temple; always they executed their royal offices from within the palace. In Ezekiel we have the Messiah coming into the Third Temple on the Day of the Lord and ruling from there on his throne.

"These verses," he continued, "categorically state that at the time of Christ's triumphant return to his Temple, gifts will be brought to Mount Zion—gifts from Ethiopia. Furthermore, these gifts will be brought to Mount Zion to the place of the 'Name of the Lord Almighty.'"

In Scripture, the place of the "Name of the Lord" has always been closely associated with the holy Temple. Moreover, by tracing this phrase from Deuteronomy to Jeremiah, this place where the Lord's name could forever be found occupied the space directly above the Ark of the Covenant within the Holy of Holies.

"What?" I was aware that such a place also described the space between the wings of the cherubim on the mercy seat. "Ken—what are you getting at?"

He turned back to the Old Testament and explained how the place of God's name changed over time, from a broader to a more specific usage, as God narrowed and refined the order and method of the "place of My Name." Throughout the Old Testament, the passages did not refer merely to the Temple but to the Holy of Holies within the Temple.

"The Hebrew of this word—*gifts*—actually translates as 'gift.' It is singular, Bob. If I'm reading this right, one very important gift will be brought out of Ethiopia at the return of Christ. The gift couldn't simply be a sacrifice, since sacrifices have always been made in the Temple courtyard, outside the inner sanctum. No, it seems from many Scriptures that a gift—singular—would come into the Temple. Isaiah 18 makes it clear that the gift would travel north from Ethiopia to Jerusalem sometime after Christ's return and end up inside the Holy Place of the messianic Temple in a place located distinctly 'between the cherubim,' above the Ark itself."

I was silent. Bold, colorful images of monks marching from Ethiopia in procession to Jerusalem with some ultimate, incomparable gift filled my imagination. I had never heard or read of such an event in all my travels or research. I started thinking about the joyous and loud Timkat celebrations I had seen.

Spellbound, I barely heard Ken's next question, which he asked as slowly and deliberately as he could. "Bob, what is the only gift that could be worthy of being placed in the Holy of Holies of the messianic Temple?"

"The Ark of the Covenant," I replied.

"Exactly."

During the following weeks, the more we tried to discount the Ark in Ethiopia theory, the more evidence we unearthed that something significant would come from Ethiopia to occupy the Most Holy Place in the messianic Temple. The Ark may have a profound role to play in future events.

It turned out, much to our amazement, that Scripture contained many references to these events. The book of Zephaniah, for example, says, "From beyond the rivers of Ethiopia My worshipers, the daughter of My dispersed ones, shall bring My offering" (Zephaniah 3:10).

The offering described by Zephaniah is also singular. God's worshippers will bring him a gift. Even more intriguing than the imagery of the gift is the Hebrew meaning of the word *bring*. The term in

Zephaniah 3:10 doesn't indicate a typical offering. The word *yabal*—cited in both Isaiah 18 and Zephaniah 3—differs vastly from the common term *bo* in that it implies a bringing or leading forth in an official or royal procession (Psalm 68:29; Isaiah 18:7). There will be a procession from Cush bringing something of great importance to Jerusalem from beyond the rivers of Ethiopia.

Scripture was telling us that some incredibly significant event would follow Jesus' glorious entrance into Jerusalem. That event, it appeared, involved a royal procession from Ethiopia to present the Messiah with a gift of great importance. This gift would be brought into the very place where his name dwells forever—into the Holy of Holies of the Jerusalem Temple.

Given my own long-simmering assumptions about Ethiopia, it didn't require a huge leap for me to speculate on what that singular gift might be. What could be worthy of being brought all the way inside the Temple to the Messiah—especially since traditional offerings are always received outside the Temple?

What, indeed, other than the Ark of the Covenant?

THE THRONE

My days and nights blended together. I was excited and frightened. I was now intruding on the misty realm of future events described in the Bible. I was treading on the unfamiliar ground of biblical prophecy, and for me it was unsure footing, yet I was drawn by the possibilities. I decided to use the Bible as I always had and let the words of the Bible itself guide me through the smoky chambers of the prophets.

From the gray glow of my computer screen emerged a much deeper mystery than I could have imagined. I saw the unfolding panorama of a gold Ark being carried on poles by Hebrew priests from the Levitical Jews who now live on the shore of Lake T'ana. They would bring it as a gift to the Temple in Jerusalem, which according to the passage in Ezekiel that Ken Durham had shown me, is the place of Christ's throne.

"Son of man, this is the place of My throne and the place of the soles of My feet, where I will dwell in the midst of the children of Israel forever." (Ezekiel 43:7)

Ezekiel's words speak of Christ's throne in the Temple—the same Temple that the gift from Ethiopia will occupy. These throne metaphors keep appearing, and they seem to be more than just metaphors. They look suspiciously like facts about the future.

Zechariah, for example, provides a stirring account of the returning King as he reigns from his throne in the Temple:

From His place He shall branch out, and He shall build the temple of the Lord; yes, He shall build the temple of the Lord. He shall bear the glory, and shall sit and rule on His throne; so He shall be a priest on His throne, and the counsel of peace shall be between them both. (Zechariah 6:12-13)

Verses like these, and many others, seem to portray the mercy seat of the Ark as a throne. I began directing my gaze toward scriptural references to God's throne and considering the mercy seat as something separate and distinct from the Ark of the Covenant. During Israel's wandering in the wilderness, the mercy seat (as God's throne) shone through from the Ark's earliest appearance. The image lingered as God spoke to Moses in the Tabernacle.

> *Now when Moses went into the tabernacle of meeting to speak with Him, he heard the voice of One speaking to him from above the mercy seat that was on the ark of the Testimony, from between the two cherubim; thus He spoke to him. (Numbers 7:89)*

Some time later, when God had established the Hebrews in the land of Israel, David moved the Tabernacle to the City of David, where the Ark and the mercy seat became the heart of Solomon's Temple, located on the Temple Mount in Jerusalem. King Solomon recounts this in 1 Kings, memorializing the plans of his father, David, to build a Temple for the Lord and saying, "I have built a house for the name of the Lord God of Israel. And there I have made a place for the ark, in which is the covenant of the Lord which He made with our fathers, when He brought them out of the land of Egypt" (1 Kings 8:20-21).

Solomon then called for the installation of the Ark as God's throne in the newly constructed Temple, praying, "Now therefore, arise, O Lord God, to Your resting place, You and the ark of Your strength" (2 Chronicles 6:41). Following Solomon's prayer, God consumed the sacrifices that had been offered, and "the glory of the Lord filled the temple. And the priests could not enter the house of the Lord, because the glory of the Lord had filled the Lord's house" (2 Chronicles 7:1-2).

Centuries later, Jesus would use the same imagery when he spoke prophetically of the Son of Man (Jesus himself) coming "in His glory, and all the holy angels with Him," adding, "then He will sit on the throne of His glory" (Matthew 25:31). As incredible as it sounded, the biblical evidence kept mounting to commend the mercy seat of the Ark as the literal, physical throne of the coming Messiah.

All of these facets come together beautifully in Psalm 132.

> *Arise, O Lord, to Your resting place, You and the ark of Your strength. Let Your priests be clothed with righteousness, and let Your saints shout for joy. For Your servant David's sake, do not turn away the face of Your Anointed. The Lord has sworn in truth to David; He will not turn from it: "I will set upon your throne the fruit of your body. If your sons will keep My covenant and My testimony which I shall teach them, their sons also shall sit upon your throne forevermore." For the Lord has chosen Zion; He has desired it for His habitation: "This is My resting place forever; here I will dwell, for I have desired it." (Psalm 132:8-14)*

These words have traveled across the ages to show us future events. In the most moving terms, these words say that the Lord's resting place is with the Ark of his strength (Psalm 132:8) in the Holy of Holies. God the Father will place the fruit of David's body (Jesus) to rule forever (Psalm 132:11). The Messiah will sit on the throne in precisely the same place occupied by the Ark of his strength—that is, the Ark of the Covenant.

MOSAIC ON THE FLOOR

I started to see these Bible verses as a vast mosaic of tiny colored pieces of glass spread out on the floor. Each verse clarified the unfolding image. I started to record what I saw as cryptic messages from the prophets into my computer. For instance, in the wilderness wanderings, Moses always said three distinct phrases whenever the priest moved the Ark: "Rise up, O Lord! Let Your enemies be scattered, and let those who hate You flee before You" (Numbers 10:35).

Almost identical versions of these three phrases are found in Psalm 68. The cryptic message from other verses in this psalm caught my attention. "They have seen Your procession, O God, the procession of my God, my King, into the sanctuary" (v. 24). "Because of Your temple at Jerusalem, kings will bring presents to You" (v. 29). "Ethiopia will quickly stretch out her hands to God" (v. 31).

I knew we were standing on a radical new theory that would not sit well with many traditionalists. Bible verses kept mounting. The verse that caused me the most excitement came from the New Testament.

In the book of Acts, Luke records a significant encounter between one of Christ's followers and a eunuch from Ethiopia. The event occurred shortly after Christ's death and resurrection.

Following the Holy Spirit's outpouring on the Day of Pentecost and Christianity's first dramatic conversions, the early church swelled with new believers. Thousands came to faith in an atmosphere of miracles, signs, and marvelous wonders. The revival shook the religious leaders of the day, who regarded the followers of Christ as a threat. Severe persecution broke out, scattering Christians throughout Judea and Samaria. Yet the persecution only galvanized the new believers, who "preached the word wherever they went" (Acts 8:4, NIV).

One such preaching witness was a man named Philip. He had traveled to Samaria to preach the message of Christ and work miraculous signs. Many conversions accompanied his sermons. In the course of his powerful missionary tour, an angel of the Lord appeared and instructed Philip to "go south to the road—the desert road—that goes down from Jerusalem to Gaza" (Acts 8:26, NIV). There the apostle met an Ethiopian eunuch returning home from Jerusalem.

Luke, the writer of Acts, identifies the Ethiopian as a prominent official in the court of Candace, queen of the Ethiopians. The man managed her royal treasury and had come to Jerusalem (this terminology matches that used by Matthew in referring to the journey of the magi to honor and submit to the Messiah in Matthew 2:2).

The eunuch had begun his journey home when Philip, guided by the Holy Spirit, ran up to his chariot and overheard the eunuch reading from Isaiah 53. The passage (Isaiah 53:7-8) foretold the crucifixion of Christ. Most Christians know the rest of the story. Philip asked the eunuch if he understood what he read. Informed of the man's perplexity, Philip told the Ethiopian the Good News of Christ. The encounter ended with the eunuch professing faith in the Savior, being baptized by Philip, and starting home to Africa in high spirits (Acts 8:39). Suddenly the Spirit whisked Philip away, and the Ethiopian returned to Cush, no doubt, to sow the seeds of Christianity throughout the Aksumite kingdom.

The story gives us a wonderful glimpse of a telling moment in the expansion of the church into northern Africa. But here we have to ask, Is there more to Luke's story? What if we dared to view the entire episode in a slightly different light—say, from the context of Isaiah 18—recalling that centuries earlier, Isaiah foresaw some great offering coming forth from Ethiopia at the Messiah's triumphant return. By adjusting the slide under this microscope, we might see an otherwise minor passage come into sharp focus. Seen through the lens of Isaiah 18, Philip's encounter on the desert road may be extremely significant.

WHY DID HE COME?

We know that the eunuch had charge of all of Candace's treasures (Acts 8:27). But why, other than to worship, had this particular Ethiopian traveled to Jerusalem? And why had Luke bothered to record it? Why did Candace send a eunuch, and why did he carry in his chariot a cumbersome scroll of Isaiah? Finally, why did Philip decide to walk beside the chariot as the eunuch read from Isaiah 53? Could this episode shed light on the question of whether the Ark and the mercy seat resided in Ethiopia at that time?

The answers we propose might come as a shock. They are triggered by the following verses:

> *The Lord has made bare His holy arm in the eyes of all the nations; and all the ends of the earth shall see the salvation of our God. Depart! Depart! Go out from there, touch no unclean thing; go out from the midst of her, be clean, you who bear the vessels of the Lord. (Isaiah 52:10-11)*

The phrase "Go out from there . . . you who bear the vessels of the Lord" seems to shine like a neon light. The phrase immediately precedes Isaiah 53, which prophesies Christ's suffering and death. No doubt the Ethiopian viewed Isaiah 52 and 53 as they should be—as two parts of a whole. Could he have received them as marching orders to make haste to Jerusalem to behold the Messiah?

Could this verse be a clue alerting us to the eunuch's true motives for visiting Jerusalem and for the Holy Spirit's urgent insistence that Philip approach the chariot? If the Ark and mercy seat indeed lay hidden in northern Ethiopia, then no doubt both articles (or "vessels of the Lord") had been registered among Candace's royal treasury. And if the monarch of Ethiopia considered those vessels a holy trust to be held until the arrival of Israel's Messiah, then the eunuch's purpose in visiting Jerusalem may well have been to determine whether the throne would now be required. Could the royal emissary of those "who bear the vessels of the Lord" have gone to Jerusalem to determine the identity of the Messiah? Because eunuchs were considered clean, the Ethiopian emissary would qualify as one who could bear the "vessels of the Lord" as described in Isaiah 52.

This interpretation meshes neatly with our theory of the Ark coming forth in royal procession from Ethiopia at Christ's second coming to the messianic Temple in Jerusalem, where it would serve as the throne of Christ in the Most Holy Place.

CHALLENGES TO THE THEORY

In proposing a new theory, one must always address troublesome verses that may waylay the idea. Jeremiah 3:16 seems to mangle the whole theory of the Ark residing in Ethiopia:

> "In those days, when your numbers have increased greatly in the land," declares the Lord, "men will no longer say, 'The ark of the covenant of the Lord.' It will never enter their minds or be remembered; it will not be missed, nor will another one be made." (NIV)

Taken in isolation, this verse seems to indicate that in the future no one will care about the Ark of the Covenant. It will not even be missed. But the next verse makes the difference:

> At that time Jerusalem shall be called The Throne of the Lord, and all the nations shall be gathered to it, to the name of the Lord, to Jerusalem. (Jeremiah 3:17)

The Ark of the Covenant, the wooden box that held the law, will no longer be the focus. It has done its job in history; it held the law and will be of little importance to future events. But the mercy seat—the solid-gold lid that crowned the Ark—is divinely designed with a prophetic obligation. If our theory is correct, the mercy seat will be used as a throne in the Temple of the Lord. The very place where the blood offering was placed as a sin offering in Old Testament times is the same place from which Christ will rule in Jerusalem as all nations gather to worship him.

According to 2 Samuel 6:2, the mercy seat is where God sat "enthroned." Early on, Scripture differentiates the mercy seat from the Ark proper:

> "You shall put the mercy seat on top of the ark, and in the ark you shall put the Testimony that I will give you. And there I will meet with you, and I will speak with you from above the mercy seat, from between the two cherubim which are on the ark of the Testimony, of all things which I will give you in commandment to the children of Israel." (Exodus 25:21-22)

The end of the matter is simply this: if what lies in Aksum is the true Ark, then God's protective hand is upon it. It will not be moved, seen, or touched before its time. God will do what God will do, directing events for his own pleasure, at his own discretion, to his own ends, sometimes in cooperation with, but often in spite of, what humans think or do. One day when the Messiah's banner is raised on the mountains of Israel and his trumpet sounds, God's holy offering will rise from the nation of strange speech, from the land divided by rivers, from Ethiopia. At that time, a gift will be brought to Mount Zion, to the place of the name of the Lord of Hosts in the Holy of Holies.

A DIFFERENCE OF PERSPECTIVE

Narud sat in silence after Godefa interpreted our last words on the theory of the throne of Christ. We had taken him step-by-step through our thinking. I was certain that he would be impressed with the idea and with the special role Ethiopia would play in future events.

Instead, Narud shook his head and said no. He was firm on the subject but not upset, confused, or offended. Narud believed what he believed; his faith was more ensconced in centuries of tradition. He, like most Ethiopians, believed that the Ark came to Ethiopia, but arrived during the reign of Solomon and not later, as we believed. The Ethiopian legend states that the illegitimate son of the queen of Sheba and Solomon took the Ark from the temple in Jerusalem and carried it to Aksum.

I confronted Narud with the fact that Aksum didn't even exist until a later date, but he seemed indifferent to my comment. I then told Narud that the Ark was in the Temple in 701 BC when Hezekiah was praying to the Lord who dwells between the cherubim above the Ark and that this event occurred almost three centuries after Solomon.

Narud simply said that the dates were wrong and that the Ark was taken by Menelik. With that, the meeting was over. He said good-bye, and we walked into the dark street.

I could tell that Godefa was troubled. He looked up into the black sky washed in brilliant stars. He stared as if he were peering into the heavens for some kind of an answer. This young deacon would in all likelihood some day be the keeper of the Ark, or it might rest in his control as Administrator. For more than two thousand years, his forefathers had believed that God had divinely entrusted them with the care of the Ark of the Covenant. He seemed confused about what to say to Chuck and me.

He looked at us with the trace of a smile and said, "I believe you are right. The time may come when the Ark will rise again and be carried to its resting place in Jerusalem. It was not the appropriate time when our Ethiopian eunuch went to Jerusalem two thousand years ago. When it is the appointed hour, we will return the Ark to its final resting place in the Temple in Jerusalem, but until then we will remain the keepers of the holy Ark."

I had delivered a message found hidden in the pages of the Bible to a young man who may one day make the important decision to pass this information on to his successor about the day when the Messiah's banner will be raised on the mountains of Israel and his trumpet sounds.

At that time, he will bring the gift to Mount Zion, to the place of the name of the Lord of Hosts.

Bahar Dar, Ethiopia, 2004

Late one morning in July 2004, our boat pulled away from the dock
at Bahar Dar one last time. We headed across the immense Lake
T'ana, which was gorged to the brim by a week of steady rain, its
normally lime-colored water a muddy copper. A small flock of
white pelicans glided out of the haze and drifted low across our
bow, their drooping bellies etching frothy white lines in the still
water. Along the shoreline to my left, the dense jungle was alive
with brightly colored birds cawing, screeching, and darting about
in the tangled brush. One dead tree towered above the rest, its
huge, barren limbs twisting skyward as if attempting to scratch
away the morning mist.

It was hard to believe that six years ago I had headed out across these waters on my first trip to T'ana Kirkos Island, the Ethiopian holy island of the golden Ark. Back then I was with Joby Book and Misgana on a small skiff; now I was on a large boat with a film crew doing a story on the Ark for the History Channel. Misgana was still my guide, and I could think of no better man for the job. He had been my trusted companion since the beginning of my search for the Ark. As the big boat chugged north across the lake, Misgana was all smiles. I had brought him good business over the years, and now he was arranging the travel for a major cable network. He sat next to me in the stern and looked my way with appreciative eyes that silently said thank you.

An hour into our three-hour cruise, I asked Misgana to point out the island where he grew up. He lifted his arm and pointed west to a distant slate-gray knob of land.

"What was your childhood like?" I asked. Even though we had come to know each other well, I had never heard him speak of his boyhood.

Misgana drew in a breath and gazed at his distant island home. His smile disappeared. He said nothing for minutes, and then he shrugged his shoulders. He looked as though he had wilted under the question.

"Misgana, are you all right?" I was afraid that my simple question had been too personal.

He turned to me, looking wounded. The problem with painful memories is that years never dull their sharp edges. "Military jets streaked across the skies over the lake daily. It was a frightening sound to a little boy. A civil war was raging all around, bombs were dropping, and helicopter gunships shot rockets into the hills. Machine guns clattered through the night as I lay trembling on my bamboo mat all alone in the dark. Many of my friends died or were carried off to fight in the war. I never saw them again."

Misgana cleared his throat and continued on. "During the war, if you were found to be subversive to the government, the soldiers would drag you out of your house and shoot you on the spot. Then the soldiers would go to your family and force them to pay for the bullets they had just used. When I was fifteen years old, they took me from my house and bound my hands tightly behind me. I was taken to a military camp and trained to fight with a machine gun. We had to sit together on a concrete floor all night when not training to be soldiers. We were only allowed to use the toilet once a day, and that was in the evening. As we sat on the cold, filthy floor, they forced us to sing patriotic songs saying that we were happy to die for our mother country. If I didn't sing with enough enthusiasm, they would take me out and beat me with a stick."

I had expected stories of young men playing in the trees, fishing on the shore, or learning a trade. Instead, I was reminded that the most beautiful of countries could never hide the ugliness of humanity. I could see that Misgana was unable to mask his pain and sensed that the worst of his ordeal was still to be spoken.

"Stop," I said. "You don't need to relive that."

"Oh, Mr. Bob," Misgana said, "there is no more war for us today." He then lifted his face heavenward as the brilliant sun slid from behind a bank of dark clouds and said, "God saved me, and all is well now."

As the boat continued to push through the lake, I had the distinct feeling that of the two of us, he was the better man.

Two hours later the boat nudged a pile of rocks and docked below the sheer granite wall of T'ana Kirkos. Young monks in tattered robes greeted us and led our group along the path and up some stone steps to the top of the cliff, where my old friend Abba hobbled up to welcome me. He flung his shawl over his right shoulder and embraced me. The strong scent of incense rose from his robe. He kissed each cheek five or six times, a sign of deep affection at my returning to his island.

Abba then greeted the film crew and proudly led us on a tour, first stopping at the rock ridge where legend says that the Ark sat in a tent for eight hundred years. Then he showed us the grave of the ancient Levite priest who brought the Ark to T'ana Kirkos four hundred years before Christ was born. The grave was aboveground in a makeshift mausoleum wedged between two big boulders in a V formation. According to Abba, the priest was laid to rest in the bottom of the split, and rocks were placed over him. Because some rocks had recently fallen away, I stooped to see if anything new was exposed, but all I could see were spiderwebs.

On the way back to our campsite, Abba said we would be allowed to film the island treasures in the morning. The film crew was excited to see the amazing relics that were purported to be from the Temple in Jerusalem. I was a little complacent about seeing the artifacts again, since I had inspected them several times before.

We settled into our tents for the night as a nasty storm blew in from the west. The pummeling rain was accompanied by frequent streaks of lightning. The thunder resonated off the water like howitzers. Water dripped inside my "waterproof" tent, and the floor was soon soaked. I wrapped my computer in a plastic bag and settled on top of the big sponge that had been my sleeping bag to sleep poorly.

I was awakened at 4:00 AM by the hollow thumping of cowskin

drums in the old church. The monks sang a repeated muffled chorus of *"Vummm yummm ahhhh vummm,"* accompanied by the deep base of the thumping percussion. The rain had stopped, but I was cold, wet, and miserable. Further sleep was futile, so I decided to warm up by taking a walk. I dressed, pounded the bugs out of my boots, slipped my jacket on, and grabbed my flashlight. The narrow beam of light followed the monks' bare footprints in the mud that led to the island's crumbling sanctuary. As I passed by the church, I could see the incense smoke seeping out of the walls by the yellow light of the candles glowing inside. I wandered for a while until I came to the cliff where the monks believed that the Ark had once sat.

I walked by the ancient altar of cut stone where the blood sacrifices were performed and continued up the trail to the rock-pile grave of the Levite priest. I shined my flashlight into the wet rocks and tried to see inside, but as on the day before, all I could see were matted yellow spiderwebs and dead weeds. I pushed at the tangled webs with a stick and was surprised when several loose rocks tumbled into the oozing mud. With a little effort, some bigger rocks also pulled free. About fourteen inches in, I had an opening the size of my fist into the rock tomb. I stuck my light inside and tried to see.

With some maneuvering of the beam, I could make out an inner cavity where the body had lain. It was about a foot high, a foot and a half wide, and approximately six feet long. The light cast from the flashlight against the dangling webs made eerie, moving shadows, and agitated spiders scurried about. The grave was empty except for a few fragments of what I took to be brown bits of bone and pottery shards. It had been almost two and a half millennia since anyone had looked at the Ark courier. He was now within my arm's reach, but there was almost nothing left of him. The humid African jungle and centuries of roaming insects had ravaged his remains.

My mind swirled. Were these the dusty remains of a Levite priest who brought the Ark to T'ana Kirkos so long ago? I slid my arm into the tight opening and groped blindly in hope of getting a broken piece of pottery. My straining fingers closed on something. As a creature scurried across my forearm, I yanked my hand back and retreated several steps. My heart was doing triple time, but at least I held something in my hand. I stuffed the pottery shard into my jacket. I had had enough of mud, spiders, and other crawling things. I went back to my tent and tried to get some rest, but sleep eluded me. I waited for the film crew to wake at dawn.

After breakfast, we met Abba in front of the treasury, a thick rock-and-mud-wall structure with a thatched roof. Abba carefully pulled a string of keys from under his cloak. One at a time, he unlocked the three locks securing the door to the treasury and slid back the bolts. The heavy wooden doors creaked open, and the treasures of the island were brought out and displayed one by one. First the blood basin called a *gomer* was brought out, then the meat forks for the burnt offering ceremony, a large grate upon which animals were sacrificed, and the meat hooks for hanging the slaughtered animals. The monks said that these implements were used in the ancient Hebrew blood sacrifices.

The film crew set up their cameras and interviewed me while shooting video of all the artifacts. I was stunned when a young monk entered the dark treasury and brought out an object that I was unaware of. Even Abba seemed surprised that the monk brought it out, but he allowed it. It was a harness of flattened and corroded metal with shoulder straps that supported two metal bands that went around the rib cage. It wasn't armor because it was so thin; it was . . .

My mind froze. I had a sudden thought but my rational mind was balking at the idea. Could this be the undergarment frame that supported the ornately jeweled breastplate used by the high priest in the Holy of Holies?

The thought stunned me into silence. In any case, I had no way to prove it.

LIGHTNING STRIKES AGAIN

As we left the island headed back to port, I was amazed that every visit to this place whisked more grains of obscuring sand away from the mystery. Had the Ark been hidden in the legendary heart of Ethiopia since Old Testament times only to emerge at such a time as this?

I had much to think about, but thinking was becoming difficult. In 2000, I had endured a shipwreck caused by a fast-moving storm. Now to the northeast, dark clouds began to pile up as lightning ripped the air. *Here we go again,* I thought, as rolling swells began to pound the boat's hull. About two hours from port, the storm hit with a vengeance.

Misgana stood by me and couldn't help seeing the humor in it all. "Hey, Mister Bob. Remember our shipwreck four years ago?"

"How could I forget?" I answered.

He shook his head. "Well, the same captain is driving this boat right now."

I hadn't noticed it at first, but as I looked at the skipper I recognized him. He looked just as frightened now as he had a few years before.

As I stared at him, he glanced my way and shrugged his shoulders as if to say, *This is the last time I'm taking you on my boat.*

We closed the hatch to ride the rolling sea as we entered a silver curtain of rain. The wind howled, and thunder clapped. With nothing to do but hold on, the film crew eased the tension by swapping adventure stories.

To our relief, the storm abated. Aside from some residual fear, we were none the worse for the experience. The lake flattened out as the boat captain maneuvered past the submerged rocks that lay just inches below the surface. We could easily have sliced our hull if we had hit any of them, but there would be no such drama this time. There was only a rusty old boat full of wet, tired men. We chugged slowly up to the concrete dock, guided by the headlights of our waiting bus.

BACK TO AKSUM

The next day we went to Aksum, the final shooting location of the show. We had not planned it, but on the morning we were to begin shooting, the holy day of Mehila began. At 4:30 AM, the *tabot* rode out of Saint Mary of Zion Church on the shoulders of the priests. I was surprised, because I was unaware that the ornate ceremonial box was brought out on any other day of the year besides the celebration of Timkat.

The host of the show (Josh) and I were handed traditional white shawls and long braided candles. We were immediately swept into the somber procession of black faces. Everyone clutched glowing amber flames; the twirling smoke hung over our heads under the sickle moon brilliant in the black sky. The cool morning air was still damp from the drenching rains of the previous night, but the rain clouds had moved on into the sur-rounding valleys.

A thousand angelic voices rose from the hearts of those around us. I looked behind to see the *tabot* on the shoulders of priests dressed in multicolored robes. Priests walking beside the *tabot* car-ried lanterns and swung incense burners, bathing the crowd of worshippers in piquant smoke and light. A young boy sprayed me with a mist of perfume.

Along the processional route, women in shawls held candles; they slowly dropped to their knees as the *tabot* passed, bowing and pressing their foreheads into the mud. Their lips moved with their prayers.

Josh is Jewish. His eyes, filled with awe, reflected a thousand burning candles. He said, "This is like the worship in biblical times. . . . This is amazing."

The faithful around us sang their prayer the entire way, repeat-ing the same melodic words over and over: *"Egziyo, meharene, Krisos."* The men sang in a hushed baritone, and the women gave the antiphonal response. The processing choir expressed a depth of worship that I had never experienced. The music was at the heart of their worship, not an add-on. I asked a monk next to me what the words meant. He said, "The people are begging, 'Forgive us all our faults, Jesus.'"

The entire pageant set the final jewel in my search for the Ark. I had never known such reverent worship. In the prepackaged world of the church with its many spoon-fed sermons and much raising of money, I had been unaware that this level of devotion existed. I felt as if I could have dropped to my knees and pressed my own face into the mud of this poor village, begging God to forgive my sins.

This was not worship of a box called the Ark, and the object carried about wrapped in red velvet was only a small replica of the Ark or possibly a copy of the Ten Commandments. The real Ark was reputably in the chapel under the steady eye of the Guardian. To the crowd, it was the very throne of God, the place where the blood of the sin offering had been placed by the high priests on the holy Day of Atonement. God has said that he will rule forever from this throne. The symbol of God's glory on earth was passing through the crowds, and like their Levite forefathers, the people bowed in worship of the unfathomable presence of the Lord in their midst.

LIFTING A CANDLE

I have followed Moses' steps across the blistering sands of Saudi Arabia, and I have chased the legends of the Ark of the Covenant through Israel, Egypt, and Ethiopia. I have logged countless miles in insufferable heat and bitter cold, endured sleepless nights in tents, sickness from bad food, fatigue, loneliness, and disappointment. Through it all, I have been blessed with the knowledge that I have stood on holy ground on the real Mount Sinai in Saudi Arabia and may actually have stood in the shadow of the Ark of the Covenant.

When I began this quest, I regarded the Old Testament as a compilation of old legends that had migrated on the winds of time. I now believe that these stories in the Bible are reliable history. The ancient scribes copied the original texts of Scripture with such scrupulous accuracy and holy reverence that we have inherited an incomparable divine literature. The evidence I have seen has convinced me that the Bible is an accurate compass, not only for revealing the past, but also for living in the present and preparing for the future. Its stories have not changed over time, nor will they change as time goes by. I am humbled and awestruck by the opportunities I have had to lift a candle into the dimly lit chambers of ancient history and see a glimpse of what has been lost in time. These truths are now deeply rooted within my heart.

NOTES

1. Stephen L. Caiger, *Bible and Spade: An Introduction to Biblical Archaeology* (London: Oxford University Press, 1936).
2. Flavius Josephus, *Antiquities of the Jews,* book II, ch. 15.
3. David Frankfurter, ed., *Pilgrimage and Holy Space in Late Antique Egypt* (Boston: Brill, Leiden, 1998).
4. G. W. B. Huntingford, trans., ed., *The Periplus of the Erythraean Sea* (London: Hakluyt Society, 1980).
5. Flavius Josephus, *The History of the Destruction of Jerusalem,* book VII, ch. 1.
6. Gaalyah Cornfeld, *Archaeology of the Bible Book by Book* (San Francisco: Harper and Row, 1976), 25, 118.
7. Graham Hancock, *The Sign and the Seal* (New York: Crown, 1992).
8. Bezaleel Porten, *Archives from Elephantine: The Life of an Ancient Jewish Military Colony* (Berkeley: University of California Press, 1968), 109, 152.
9. Edward M. Blaikloch and R. K. Harrison, eds., *New International Dictionary of Biblical Archaeology* (Grand Rapids: Zondervan, 1983), 177.

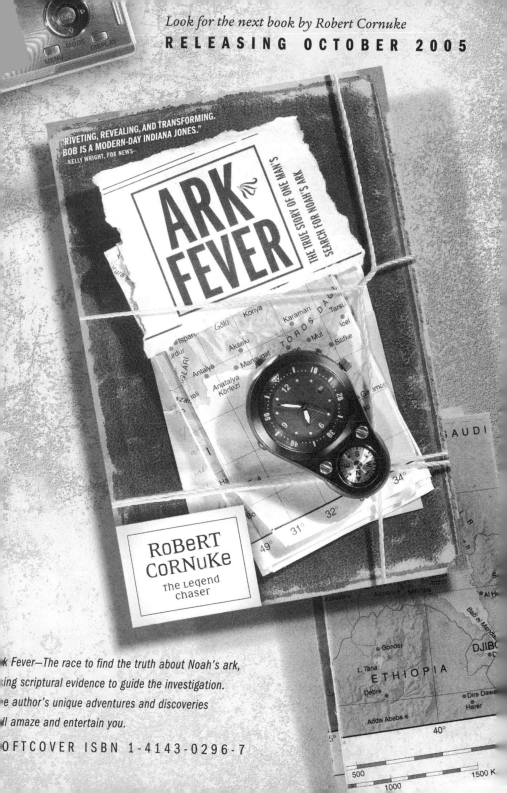

Look for the next book by Robert Cornuke

RELEASING OCTOBER 2005

"RIVETING, REVEALING, AND TRANSFORMING.
BOB IS A MODERN-DAY INDIANA JONES."
—KELLY WRIGHT, FOX NEWS—

ARK FEVER

THE TRUE STORY OF ONE MAN'S
SEARCH FOR NOAH'S ARK

ROBERT
CORNUKE
THE LEGEND
CHASER

*k Fever—The race to find the truth about Noah's ark,
ing scriptural evidence to guide the investigation.
e author's unique adventures and discoveries
ll amaze and entertain you.*

OFTCOVER ISBN 1-4143-0296-7

1. Traditional Mt. Sinai location in the lower Sinai Peninsula (Egypt) — There is absolutely no archaeological evidence to suggest that this mountain is the real Mt. Sinai. COPYRIGHT © ROBERT CORNUKE.

2. Underwater land bridge — This submerged land mass spans from the tip of the Sinai Peninsula to the Saudi Arabian coastline and is the best candidate site for the crossing point of the Hebrews through the Red Sea. COPYRIGHT © ROBERT CORNUKE.

3. Jabal al-Lawz — Ancient historians and recent archaeological discoveries suggest this mountain as the real Mt. Sinai. Note the blackened peak, which is consistent with the biblical description of God descending on the mountain in fire (see Exodus 19:18). COPYRIGHT © ROBERT CORNUKE.

4. Elijah's Cave — Elijah sought refuge in a cave on Mt. Sinai (see 1 Kings 19:8-13). Could this be the very cave where Elijah stayed? PHOTO COURTESY OF JIM AND PENNY CALDWELL. COPYRIGHT © JIM AND PENNY CALDWELL.

5. This picture is believed by the author to be the stone altar site where the Israelites worshipped the golden calf referred to in Exodus 32:1-19. COPYRIGHT © ROBERT CORNUKE.

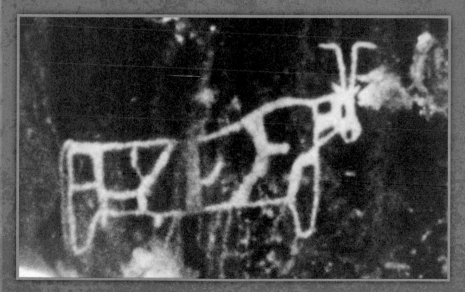

6. This ancient rock drawing inscribed on the "golden calf" altar site appears to be an Egyptian bull god. COPYRIGHT © ROBERT CORNUKE.

7. Blackened rocks on top of Jabal al-Lawz. The outer coating of these rocks has the appearance of being burnt. The Bible says that God descended on Mount Sinai in flames of a furnace. Could these be rocks charred by that holy fire? Note that the surrounding mountain peaks are all the color of tan granite. COPYRIGHT © ROBERT CORNUKE.

8. Blackened rock broken apart by the author. Note the outer layer of rock, which appears to be burnt black, in contrast to the tan granite interior. COPYRIGHT © ROBERT CORNUKE.

9. Stone monolith split from top to bottom with evidence of water erosion at its base. Was this the rock that Moses struck with his staff (see Exodus 17:6) and water gushed out for the Hebrews to drink? PHOTO COURTESY OF JIM AND PENNY CALDWELL. COPYRIGHT © JIM AND PENNY CALDWELL.

10. This picture shows evidence of a large volume of water that once came from this rock, which the author believes is the actual split rock at Horeb. This amazing find was discovered by Jim and Penny Caldwell. PHOTO COURTESY OF JIM AND PENNY CALDWELL. COPYRIGHT © JIM AND PENNY CALDWELL.

11. & 12. Pillar segments from an altar at the base of Mount Jabal al-Lawz, believed by author to be the altar where Moses set up twelve pillars and performed burnt offerings (see Exodus 24:4-5). Thick compressed ash fills the floor of this altar. Is this the 3,500-year-old altar spoken of in the Bible? PHOTO COURTESY OF JIM AND PENNY CALDWELL. COPYRIGHT © JIM AND PENNY CALDWELL.

13. This altar has two sixty-foot sections and a rock ridge down the middle. It stands exactly at the foot of the mountain, just as the Bible describes (see Exodus 24:4). Note the pillar foundations and round sections lying on the ground below the altar site. PHOTO COURTESY OF JIM AND PENNY CALDWELL. COPYRIGHT © JIM AND PENNY CALDWELL.

14. With his son, Brandon, the author inspects a stone altar block covered in thick moss lichen. This site, it is said, is where the priests poured blood into a socket hole in the top of the granite altar for subsequent sprinkling on the Ark. The Ark was reputedly kept for eight hundred years in a tent (tabernacle) at this site on the mysterious island of T'ana Kirkos. COPYRIGHT © ROBERT CORNUKE.

15. Saint Mary's of Zion Church in Axum, Ethiopia. According to the Ethiopians, the actual Ark of the Covenant is kept in dark seclusion and holy protection inside this building. COPYRIGHT © ROBERT CORNUKE.

16. This corroded bronze bowl, called a *gomer*, sits atop an ancient stand that droops from fatigue due to its age. The gomer held the blood, which was stirred to keep it from coagulating before it was poured in the granite altar stone.
COPYRIGHT © ROBERT CORNUKE.